HEROES OF HISTORY

ALAN SHEPARD

Higher and Faster

HEROES OF HISTORY

ALAN SHEPARD

Higher
and Faster

JANET & GEOFF BENGE

Emerald
Books

P.O. BOX 635, LYNNWOOD, WA 98046

Emerald Books are distributed through YWAM Publishing. For a full list of titles, including other great biographies, visit our website at www.ywampublishing.com or call 1-800-922-2143.

Library of Congress Cataloging-in-Publication Data

Benge, Janet, 1958–
  Alan Shepard : higher and faster / Janet and Geoff Benge.
    p. cm. — (Heroes of history)
  Includes bibliographical references.
  ISBN-13: 978-1-932096-41-5
  ISBN-10: 1-932096-41-8
1. Shepard, Alan B. (Alan Bartlett), 1923–1998—Juvenile literature. 2. Astronauts—United States—Biography—Juvenile literature. I. Benge, Geoff, 1954– II. Title.
  TL789.85.S5B46 2007
  629.450092—dc22
  [B]   12007025555

Alan Shepard: Higher and Faster

13 12 11 10 09 08 07   10 9 8 7 6 5 4 3 2 1

Published by Emerald Books
P.O. Box 635
Lynnwood, Washington 98046

ISBN-13: 978-1-93209-641-5
ISBN-10: 1-93209-641-8

Printed in the United States of America.

HEROES OF HISTORY
Biographies

Abraham Lincoln
Alan Shepard
Benjamin Franklin
Christopher Columbus
Clara Barton
Daniel Boone
Douglas MacArthur
George Washington
George Washington Carver
Harriet Tubman
John Adams
John Smith
Laura Ingalls Wilder
Meriwether Lewis
Orville Wright
Theodore Roosevelt
Thomas Edison
William Penn

More Heroes of History coming soon!
Unit study curriculum guides are available
for select biographies.

Available at your local bookstore or
through Emerald Books
1 (800) 922-2143

Contents

Chapter 1

You're on Your Way!

Alan Shepard was frustrated. By now his flight should have been over, but here he was still stuck on the launchpad. Problem after problem had kept the ground controllers scrambling and had pushed back the launch time. For over three hours now Alan had been strapped into his seat in a less-than-comfortable space suit. *When is this thing going to get off the ground?* he wondered.

Alan had been awakened at one thirty in the morning to begin preparations for the flight. He had showered and shaved, eaten a hearty breakfast, and been examined by a doctor before finally donning his silver space suit. He had arrived at the launchpad at 5:00 AM and stared up at the Redstone rocket, the "bird," he called it, with the Mercury capsule secured atop. The rocket was an amazing sight as it sat

9

bathed in the glow of bright spotlights in the early-morning darkness.

Moments later Alan had ridden the elevator up the gantry and made his way across the walkway to the Mercury capsule, which he had named *Freedom 7*. Fellow astronaut John Glenn had helped him into the capsule and strapped him into his seat, ready for the flight. But now it was after eight thirty, and Alan was still on the ground, still strapped in his seat. It was so frustrating.

To make matters worse, butterflies had returned to the astronaut's stomach, and rightly so. After all, Alan was sitting on top of thousands of pounds of volatile fuel. The fuel was supposed to ignite and produce a thrust that would lift him off the launch-pad, but it could just as easily explode in a mighty fireball. Plenty of rockets had done just that at various test launches. Alan had witnessed some of them firsthand. If that happened, he would have no escape. He just had to believe that Wernher von Braun and his team, who had built the Redstone rocket, had done their job properly.

The radio crackled in Alan's ear, and a controller informed him of another delay. This time an electrical inverter on the rocket needed to be replaced. More frustration.

Finally, everything seemed to be in order, and the countdown began again. Alan breathed a sigh of relief and hoped there would be no more problems or delays.

At 9:30 AM Alan heard the voice of Deke Slayton on the radio. Deke was located at Mercury Control, two miles from the launchpad, and would be the capsule communicator for the duration of the flight. Deke and Alan had become friends during their astronaut training, and the comforting sound of his friend's voice on the radio seemed to calm the butterflies in Alan's stomach.

At 9:32 AM Deke began the final countdown. Ten...Nine...Eight...Seven...Six... Alan gripped the abort handle tightly and braced his feet against the capsule floor. Five...Four...Three... *Don't screw up, Shepard,* he muttered to himself. Two...One...Zero... Ignition...

Alan could hear a rumble below him that began to grow like thunder. Then he heard Deke's voice on the radio say, "Liftoff."

Slowly, gently, Alan felt himself rising into the sky. Then the Redstone began to pick up speed.

"You're on your way!" Deke said excitedly.

And so he was. Alan could scarcely believe it. The boy born and raised in East Derry, New Hampshire, who grew up with a passion for flying was off on the ultimate flight—to space! Not only that, he was the first American to be launched beyond the earth's atmosphere. What amazing twists and turns his life had taken to bring him to this moment.

Chapter 2

Destined to Fly

You're so lucky to have a basement like this,"
Alan Shepard's friend Joe told him as the two
boys pulled open the door. Inside was a treasure
trove of tools, discarded machines, and scraps of
metal and wood.

"Luck's not a word we use in our family," Alan
replied.

And he was right. The Shepards of East Derry,
New Hampshire, did not believe in luck but in hard
work and education. The roots of Alan's family tree
stretched all the way back to the *Mayflower* and the
founding of the Massachusetts colony. Various
ancestors had then made their way inland and settled in and around East Derry, where they had
prospered, first as potato farmers and then, as the
town grew around them, as civic and business

leaders. In fact, Alan's dead grandfather Shepard, whose basement workshop Alan was allowed to use, had been the wealthiest man in town before the Great Depression struck. He owned the Derry National Bank and the Derry Electric Light Company. And even after the Depression had forced the closure of the bank, Grandpa Shepard had retained enough money to employ a full-time butler and housekeeper.

When Alan's grandfather died, Alan's grandmother, Nanzie Shepard, had simply shut the door to her husband's workshop in the basement, until Alan took an interest in the place in 1935, soon after he turned twelve. Grandpa Shepard's workshop soon became a hive of activity. With the Depression over and the future once again looking bright for America, Alan, like many boys his age, took a particularly active interest in the aviation future of the country. Aviation had come a long way since 1923, the year Alan was born. The commercial aviation industry in America was just then getting organized. That year the first night flights across the American continent were flown, using a new system of beacons to guide airplanes. As a result, the mail was able to be delivered across the country in about thirty hours, which was two to three days less than the old way of shipping the mail cross-country by train.

When Alan was three years old, Lindbergh flew across the Atlantic Ocean from New York to Paris on the first continent-to-continent nonstop flight. Tall, handsome, witty, intelligent, and daring, Lindbergh quickly became the hero of every young boy of that generation. Although Alan was too young to remember the flight, he had read every word he could about Lindbergh in books borrowed from the East Derry library.

Now, in 1936, the age of commercial passenger air travel was getting under way. In 1933 the Boeing Airplane Company had introduced the Boeing 247, one of the first modern passenger aircraft. The plane came equipped with such marvels as a retractable undercarriage, upholstered seats, and a hot-water heater, and it could carry ten passengers in relative luxury at a cruising speed of 160 miles per hour. The following year, in 1934, the Douglas Aircraft Company introduced the DC-2, a fourteen-passenger aircraft, to compete with the Boeing 247. And then in 1935 the company introduced the DC-3, the ultimate passenger airplane, which could fly from coast to coast across the United States with just one stop to refuel.

To keep up with all of the developments in aviation, Alan had formed the Airplane Model Club. The club met in Grandpa Shepard's basement workshop, where the members would discuss aviation and build model airplanes, which some of the boys hung from strings in their bedrooms. One of the members of the Airplane Model Club was Al Deale, who owned a model glider big enough for a boy to fly in. In his eagerness to experience flight for himself, Alan had convinced Mr. Deale to let him fly the glider. He and Joe pulled the craft from Mr. Deale's barn and carried it to the top of a nearby hill, where they attached the wooden-ribbed, canvas-covered wings to the fuselage. Alan then climbed into the straps that dangled the glider over his shoulders at waist height. He ran down the hill. When he thought he had gathered enough speed, he jumped into the air and waited for the glider to carry him aloft. However, things did not go quite as planned. A sudden gust of wind caught one of the wings, flipping the glider over in the air and then dashing it to the ground. Alan went rolling down the grassy side of the hill while the glider splintered into matchwood around him. Although the glider was destroyed in the accident, Alan was not hurt, except for his bruised pride.

In the spring Alan was back in his grandfather's workshop for more experimentation. Since Alan and his friends were the only ones who went down to the basement workshop, it made perfect sense to use the place as a base for activities that his parents, Renza and Bart Shepard, would not have approved of had they known about them. In the winter, Beaver Lake, at the bottom of the hill behind the Shepard home, froze over. When the ice was thick enough, some of the older boys would drive their cars out onto the lake. They would allow the younger boys to tie ropes to their bumpers and ski along behind the cars as they drove in a large oval. Alan particularly liked to participate in this activity, and his personal best skiing speed was sixty-eight miles per hour. At that speed he loved the way the icy wind whipped through his hair as the world whizzed by in his peripheral vision.

When Christmas 1937 rolled around, soon after he had turned fourteen, Alan knew just what he wanted as a Christmas present—a ride on a real airplane, whipping along through the air at nearly two hundred miles per hour. Alan had often lain in bed at night dreaming about how the world must look from ten thousand feet up and what it must be like to journey up through the clouds. To his delight, Alan's mother granted his wish. She bought the two of them round-trip tickets from Manchester, New Hampshire, to Boston, Massachusetts, on a DC-3.

In January 1938, Mr. Shepard, accompanied by Polly, Alan's sister, who was two years younger than Alan, drove Alan and his mother to the Manchester Municipal Airport, twelve miles from the family's home. The terminal building at the airport was all Alan had hoped it would be: a modern building situated alongside the paved runway, with several airplanes parked on the tarmac in front of it.

Alan could feel his heart begin to race as he and his mother passed through the double glass doors of the terminal building and out onto the tarmac, where a line had formed beside a nearby DC-3. As Alan and his mother took their place in line waiting to board the aircraft, Alan looked up at the cockpit, where he could see the pilot and copilot, headphones strung over their ears, intently checking various gauges and switches. When it was his turn to board the DC-3 through the door at the rear, Alan took a deep breath and promised himself he would remember every detail of the flight. Inside the DC-3 was even more spacious than he had imagined it would be. The walls were covered in a soft grey vinyl, and the floors were carpeted in navy blue. Alan took his seat beside the square window and peered out. A man was checking the engines and the landing gear, and several other men were loading suitcases into the luggage compartment in the rear of the airplane.

Finally, when all the passengers were aboard and seated and all the bags were stowed away, the door to the aircraft was shut. The pipe that ran from a tanker truck to the airplane was disconnected from the underside of the wing, and the truck pulled away. In a burst of smoke, the engine on the right wing burst to life, and the propeller began to spin. Moments later the engine on the left wing started up. The engines made a rumbling sound inside the plane, which was now vibrating slightly in time to the rumble of the engines. The engines began to rev faster and faster until the propellers seemed to Alan to disappear, and then the DC-3 lurched forward and began to taxi across the tarmac.

At the end of the runway the DC-3 made a 180-degree turn to face down the runway. Suddenly the engines began to rev faster and faster until the rumble inside the cabin became a high-pitched squeal. Just when Alan began to fear that the engines might fling apart, the airplane moved forward and rapidly began to gather speed—real speed, faster than skiing behind a car on the frozen lake. As the DC-3 barreled along the runway, Alan became aware that the tail had lifted off the ground and the steep aisle he had clambered up to get to his seat was now level. Moments later the main wheels of the aircraft left the ground. Alan Shepard was airborne at last.

As the DC-3 climbed into the sky, Alan was amazed at how quickly things on the ground got smaller. He saw the winding stone fences that cordoned off the fields, and the sparkling Merrimack River. Without thinking, Alan began reciting a poem to himself that he had learned in elementary school:

Up in the air and over the wall,
Till I can see so wide,
River and trees and cattle and all
Over the countryside.

The poem, written by Robert Louis Stevenson, was about a boy on a swing who imagined he could fly. Alan smiled widely. He didn't have to imagine—he really was flying! Within moments, long wisps of white cloud were streaking past the windows of the DC-3. When the plane finally got above the clouds, Alan looked down on them from above. The clouds looked like fluffy cotton balls stretched across the sky.

The DC-3 didn't stay above the clouds for long. It took only half an hour to fly to Boston—the most glorious half hour of Alan's life so far—and soon the pilot was guiding the plane in for a landing at Logan Field in Boston. Alan watched the ground get closer and closer, and then with a mighty thump that jarred the whole airplane, and a puff of smoke from the tires of the landing gear, the plane was back on the ground. Alan had spent the whole trip with his face pressed to the window.

As the DC-3 taxied to a halt in front of the terminal building at Logan Field and the door to the aircraft was opened, Alan knew that this had been only half the excitement. He and his mother disembarked the airplane and then got right in line to board another DC-3 for the return flight to Manchester. The flight back proved to be just as magical.

By the time Alan arrived home in East Derry that night, he knew one thing for sure—he was destined to fly airplanes. The question then became, How? Answering that question consumed Alan for the next few weeks. He had to find a way to get back to the Manchester airport on a regular basis so that he could watch airplanes landing and taking off. But the airport was twelve miles away through hilly countryside, too far to ride on his old, gearless bike, and there was no chance that his father would be willing to drive him there and pick him up on a regular basis.

Finally Alan decided that he needed a better set of wheels. He wanted a fancy, new five-speed bicycle like the one he had seen in the local hardware store. That was the kind of bike that he could ride on a twenty-four-mile round-trip to the airport, in sun, rain, or snow.

Alan had a newspaper delivery route, but he realized that it would take him forever to save enough money for a new bike from the money earned delivering the papers. He decided to ask his grandmother if she would buy the bicycle for him.

As soon as the conversation with his grandmother began, Alan was sorry that he had talked to her about it. His grandmother Shepard may have been one of the wealthiest women in town, but she was also the most frugal woman. Nanzie Shepard saved bits of string and the brown paper the bread came wrapped in, and she soon pointed out that she was not about to spoil one of her grandchildren at the expense of the others. However, she did make Alan a deal. She would not buy him the bicycle he desired, but she would buy him fourteen Rhode Island Red hens and a rooster. Then, in keeping with New England frugality, Alan could raise the chickens, sell eggs, and buy himself the bike.

It seemed like the money would be a long way off, but Alan decided to accept the offer. His father, who could also have easily afforded to purchase the bike for Alan, offered instead to buy the first sack of chicken feed and a feeding trough for his son's new venture.

Alan soon knew a lot about chickens. He fed them each day and waited patiently for them to begin laying eggs. Eventually the chickens did begin to produce eggs, and Alan was able to sell the eggs to friends and neighbors for twenty-nine cents a dozen. As he did so, dollar by dollar his dream of buying a new bike crept closer to becoming a reality. Finally, on February 15, 1939, a little over a year after his flight in the DC-3, Alan had finally saved enough money to purchase the bicycle. Even though it was snowing outside, he rode the bike one hundred miles during the first week he owned it.

On the first Saturday he owned the bike, Alan headed northwest to Manchester Airport. When he reached the airport, Alan joined the group of boys gathered on the side of the hill that ran alongside the runway of the airport. There, for hours, the excited boys would sit and watch airplanes landing and taking off and talk about aviation.

After doing this each Saturday for a month, Alan felt restless. He had to find a way to learn to fly, yet he knew that all the boys sitting with him on the hillside wanted the same thing. Somehow he had to make himself stand out from the others. The next Saturday, in mid-March, Alan decided to hang around the airport tarmac and see whether he could strike up a conversation with someone who worked there.

As it so happened, Carl Park, the airport manager, noticed him. "What are you doing here, son?" he asked.

Alan shot back his most confident smile and replied, "Trying to figure out a way to get a flying lesson when I don't have any money."

Carl laughed. "At least you came straight to the point. How old are you?"

"Fifteen," Alan said.

"You any good at cleaning things?"

Alan's heart thumped in his chest. Was something going to work out for him?

"Yes, sir," he answered with confidence.

"Well, then, we could make a deal," Carl said. "You can help wipe down the planes and keep the hangars tidy, and instead of paying you, I'll give you a couple of lessons. See if you have the stomach for flying. What do you say?"

Alan grinned. "You've got yourself a deal," he said, thrusting out his hand to shake on it. Then he added, "My name's Alan Shepard, from East Derry, and I'll be the best plane wiper you've ever had."

Chapter 3

Midshipman

Alan sat in the passenger seat of the Stinson Voyager airplane beside Carl Park as they circled above Manchester, New Hampshire. He kept one eye on the ground below and one on Carl, watching everything the pilot did as he guided the plane along. As they flew, Carl explained how the various controls and gauges worked, and Alan nodded intermittently. Finally Carl told Alan to put his hands on the yoke. When Alan had done so, Carl let his hands go, and Alan was in control of the Voyager. The feeling was exhilarating, like electricity pulsing through Alan's veins. Alan was finally in control of an airplane in the air! Unlike riding his bicycle, he was piloting a vehicle that could move in four dimensions. Part of the art of being a pilot was learning how to balance the plane using the various controls to keep it flying in a certain direction at a certain height and speed. Since Carl was gently nodding his head as Alan adjusted the controls, Alan guessed he was doing okay. Finally Carl again took control of the aircraft and brought the Voyager in for a landing.

No sooner had the plane landed than Alan began plotting to go up for a second flying lesson. He did a thorough job of wiping down the planes at the airport and organizing the hangars. Soon Carl asked him if he would like to help the mechanics change spark plugs and repair the fuel lines in the planes. Alan jumped at the chance. He found the new tasks easy, since he had spent so much time tinkering with machines in his grandfather's basement.

Before long, Alan was as much a fixture at the Manchester Airport as the pilots and mechanics. Everything about the place excited him, and since he was good at what he did, he was steadily given more responsibilities. Carl even allowed him to taxi the airplanes from the tarmac to the hangar.

Toward the end of 1939, Alan began to notice changes occurring at the Manchester Airport, exciting changes for a boy who loved airplanes. More and more military cargo planes were landing at the airport and being serviced there. The reason for the increased military activity at the airport was that war had broken out in Europe.

Germany, under the leadership of Adolf Hitler, had invaded Czechoslovakia and Poland, which in turn had led to Great Britain and France declaring war on Germany and her Fascist ally, Italy, in September 1939.

The war in Europe had a direct impact on Alan, who had just entered his last year of high school, as it had on all teenage boys in the United States. These young men had to prepare for the possibility of joining the war. Alan had always known that if there were ever another war, his father would want him to train at West Point and become an army officer.

Colonel Bart Shepard was proud of his army service in France during World War I. When he returned home to East Derry after the war, he had taken a job in his father's bank and poured his spare time into working his way up the ranks of the army reserves. Now Alan's father took every oppor- tunity afforded him to wear his army uniform. Also Alan's grandfather Shepard had served as a colonel in the National Guard and was aide-de-camp at the Russo-Japanese Peace Conference organized by President Teddy Roosevelt in September 1905 to bring an end to the war between Russia and Japan.

Stories of Alan's father's and grandfather's mili- tary service had been told over and over again in the Shepard home until they had become family legend. As a result it was expected that the next generation of Shepards would also serve in the army and add their own stories to the mix. However, the army had never appealed to Alan, whose father's stories of endless days of marching through the mud did nothing to inspire him. Soon the family was at an impasse over Alan's military future.

Thankfully, Mr. Shepard's older brother Fritz noticed the tension in the household when he came to visit and suggested a compromise. Why didn't Alan apply for the U.S. Naval Academy? He would never be a colonel in the army, but it would not be so bad to have an admiral in the family. In fact, Uncle Fritz reminded them that his own family had faced a similar crossroads. His son Eric, who was five years older than Alan, had joined the Marine Corps and had dreams of becoming a fighter pilot.

Alan wondered why he had not thought of joining the navy before now. It was the perfect solution. President Franklin Roosevelt had just allotted the navy the enormous sum of two billion dollars to buy airplanes that could take off and land from ships and to train pilots to fly them. Alan's mind raced with possibilities. Perhaps by the time he had been trained as a navy pilot, Americans would be fighting the German and Italian air forces as the Allies sought to gain freedom for Europe.

Motivated by the idea of joining the navy, Alan worked hard at high school throughout the year and graduated eighth in his class of fifty-five at the prestigious Pinkerton Academy. He did even better on the Naval Academy's entrance exam, coming in second for the whole state of New Hampshire. However, since Alan had skipped two grades in elementary school, he was now only sixteen years of age and was too young to be accepted into the Naval Academy.

Rather than lose his momentum while he waited to be old enough to enter the Academy, Alan, along with his parents, decided that it would be best for him to spend a year at a military prep school. His parents chose the Admiral Farragut Academy in New Jersey for him to attend. Alan arrived there in September 1940, with the looming threat that the United States would enter the war in Europe to help protect England and France from the Nazis.

Alan and his classmates at the Admiral Farragut Academy carefully followed events in Europe as well as the rise of Japanese aggression in the Pacific region. Then, early one March morning in 1941, the reality of what could happen hit home for all of the students. The U.S. Navy ship *Reuben James* was escorting a convoy of British ships bringing vital supplies from the United States to Great Britain when the convoy was intercepted by a German submarine and fired upon. The *Reuben James* was hit by a German torpedo and sank quickly. One hundred forty-four navy men were aboard the ship, and only forty-four of them survived. The *Reuben James* was the first U.S. Navy vessel lost during World War II.

Alan studied hard at the Admiral Farragut Academy, with the goal of entering the Naval Academy the following year. His hard work paid off. On June 19, 1941, he was ordered to report to Annapolis, Maryland, the home of the Naval Academy. Arriving at the Academy was a jarring experience for Alan, who was still small for his age and one of the youngest men in his class. At seventeen he was still very much a scrawny boy, while many of the other recruits were hardened young men.

Alan's first day at the U.S. Naval Academy was hellish. All three thousand students attending the Academy, or midshipmen as they were called, lived in Bancroft Hall, an enormous five-story, ivy-covered building that contained over five miles of hallways. Bancroft Hall had eight wings that were arranged as if they were on a ship, with the even-numbered wings on the "port" side and odd-numbered wings on the "starboard" side. The five stories were referred to as "decks." Rather than using the regular hallways to get from room to room, the new recruits, or plebes as they were known, were herded down into the labyrinth of damp, narrow tunnels in the basement of the building and told to find their way from one registration point to the next.

Bancroft Hall was so extensive that it housed its own medical and dental clinics, general store, and travel office. Alan's first stop was the medical clinic where he passed a stringent physical examination. Then it was back through the basement tunnels to another room, where Alan was issued a midshipman's uniform, which reminded him of white pajamas. Then it was on to the barbershop, where Alan's hair was clipped down to a stubble. As Alan and the other plebes went from point to point, they were harassed endlessly by upperclassmen, who shouted in their faces, abused them for looking up, and generally taunted them. Then at dinner Alan learned a whole new set of "traditions." Plebes had to balance on the edge of their chairs as they ate, and they had to eat very slowly, chewing each mouthful thoroughly before swallowing. And when any upperclassman called, "Fire in the paint locker," all the plebes had to dive under the table, where the upperclassmen would throw milk or ice water on them to "douse" the fire.

Such treatment made Alan furious, but he vowed not to let the upperclassmen know how much it bothered him. By the time he retired to his bunk that first night, Alan was mentally and physically exhausted. He began to wonder why he had signed up for four years of such treatment. He hoped the following day would be better. Alas, it turned out to be just as harassing. It was the first day of class, and there was a whole new set of meaningless rules to follow. The plebes were rudely awakened at 4:30 AM, half an hour before anyone else, in order to close the windows in the dorm rooms of the upper-classmen so that they would not be too cold when they awoke. Then it was down to the dining room to learn the menu for the day so that they could relay it to the other students.

Before breakfast they had other duties as well, such as making their beds with identical exactness and shining their shoes until their white uniforms reflected in them. This was the only thing, so far, about the Academy that reminded Alan of home.

Getting to class was like running a gauntlet. The plebes had to march down the middle of the corridors in single file, being careful to make a precision turn at each corner. And they had to step aside and salute every upperclassman who passed and could be ordered at any time to drop to the ground and do push-ups.

Chafing at such treatment, Alan plotted revenge. One morning, not long after arriving at the Academy, he talked a group of plebes into hiding the left shoe of every upperclassman whose window they closed in the early hours of the morning. It was fun watching the upperclassmen scrambling around hunting for their shoes, but one of the other plebes identified Alan as the ringleader of the prank, and Alan was singled out for punishment. He was told to bend over and hold his ankles while each of those whose shoes had been taken took turns beating his backside with a broom handle.

The punishment hurt, of course, but if it was meant to make Alan any more respectful of his elders, it did not work. Soon he was "going over the wall," which meant creeping out of his dorm in the middle of the night and climbing the stone wall that encircled the Academy so that he could enjoy the nightlife in Annapolis.

Even though Alan received many letters from his father encouraging him to study hard, he found that there were too many distractions to study. Since the U.S. Naval Academy was located on the Severn River, which flowed into Chesapeake Bay at Annapolis, Alan found himself spending more and more time on the water. He became an accomplished sailor, sailing everything from a small knockabout to a ninety-foot schooner named *Freedom.* And then during his second year at the Academy, he joined the rowing team, spending hours in the gym toughening himself up to compete for a position on the team.

But no matter what Alan was doing, his mind—and the minds of all the other cadets in the Academy—was never far from thoughts of war. Things were not going well for Britain and France and their allies in Europe. Germany had captured and occupied Denmark and Norway, as well as Belgium, the Netherlands, and Luxembourg, before launching its assault on France. This led to the fall of that country in June 1940, which in turn led to the mass evacuation to England of Allied troops from Dunkirk in France. And in Asia the Japanese continued their expansion, pushing farther into China and on into Indochina as well as various Pacific islands.

Then just before 8:00 AM on Sunday, December 7, 1941, an event occurred in Hawaii that would change Alan Shepard's life and the lives of many young men his age. That day four hundred Japanese fighter planes swooped in from the north and began attacking Pearl Harbor on the Hawaiian island of Oahu, catching the American forces there off guard. Eight U.S. battleships lay at anchor in the harbor, and within minutes of the beginning of the attack, five of them were sunk or sinking fast. The remaining three were badly damaged. Three destroyers also went down, and three cruisers were damaged. At the nearby airfield, 188 Hawaii-based combat aircraft, most of which did not have time to get airborne, were smashed beyond repair by Japanese bombs. When the smoke from the two-hour attack finally cleared, over 2,400 Americans were dead and over 1,200 were wounded.

As news of the attack at Pearl Harbor was reported over the radio, Americans became united in their call for the country to enter the war. Alan noticed a distinct change at the U.S. Naval Academy when news of the attack reached the institution. Officers strapped on their sidearms, and rumors began to fly about what would happen next. The next day Alan learned what the United States' response would be to the Japanese attack.

Just after noon on Monday, December 8, Alan stood at attention in the Yard, which the grounds of the Naval Academy were called, and listened to a radio message delivered by President Franklin Roosevelt. The radio reception was loud and clear, and the president's voice was firm and resolved as he spoke.

Mr. Vice President, and Mr. Speaker, and Members of the Senate and House of Representatives: Yesterday, December 7, 1941—a date which will live in infamy—the United States of America was suddenly and deliberately attacked by naval and air forces of the Empire of Japan.

The United States was at peace with that Nation and, at the solicitation of Japan, was still in conversation with its Government and its Emperor looking toward the mainte- nance of peace in the Pacific. Indeed, one hour after Japanese air squadrons had com- menced bombing in the American Island of Oahu, the Japanese Ambassador to the

United States and his colleague delivered to our Secretary of State a formal reply to a recent American message. And while this reply stated that it seemed useless to continue the existing diplomatic negotiations, it contained no threat or hint of war or of armed attack.

It will be recorded that the distance of Hawaii from Japan makes it obvious that the attack was deliberately planned many days or even weeks ago. During the intervening time the Japanese Government has deliberately sought to deceive the United States by false statements and expressions of hope for continued peace.

The attack yesterday on the Hawaiian Islands has caused severe damage to American naval and military forces. I regret to tell you that very many American lives have been lost. In addition American ships have been reported torpedoed on the high seas between San Francisco and Honolulu.

Yesterday the Japanese Government also launched an attack against Malaya.

Last night Japanese forces attacked Hong Kong.

Last night Japanese forces attacked Guam.

Last night Japanese forces attacked the Philippine Islands.

Last night the Japanese attacked Wake Island.

And this morning the Japanese attacked Midway Island.

Japan has, therefore, undertaken a surprise offensive extending throughout the Pacific area. The facts of yesterday and today speak for themselves. The people of the United States have already formed their opinions and well understand the implications to the very life and safety of our Nation.

As Commander in Chief of the Army and Navy, I have directed that all measures be taken for our defense.

But always will our whole Nation remember the character of the onslaught against us.

No matter how long it may take us to overcome this premeditated invasion, the American people, in their righteous might, will win through to absolute victory. I believe that I interpret the will of the Congress and of the people when I assert that we will not only defend ourselves to the uttermost but will make it very certain that this form of treachery shall never again endanger us.

Hostilities exist. There is no blinking at the fact that our people, our territory, and our interests are in grave danger.

With confidence in our armed forces, with the unbounding determination of our people, we will gain the inevitable triumph. So help us God.

I ask that the Congress declare that since the unprovoked and dastardly attack by

Japan on Sunday, December 7, 1941, a state of war has existed between the United States and the Japanese Empire.

There was a moment of silence when President Roosevelt stopped speaking. Then the Yard erupted into deafening cheers of the midshipmen, Alan Shepard among them.

When the cheers finally died down, the superintendent of the Academy, Rear Admiral Russell, made his own announcement. Because the United States of America was now officially at war, the class of 1945, of which Alan was a part, would now become the class of 1944. The cadets would cram the next three years of study into two and graduate a year early!

Chapter 4

Time to Get Serious

Upon hearing that the next three years of school-
ing were to be crammed into two, Alan realized
that he and his fellow plebes would be expected to
work twice as hard to get through their workload in
the allotted time. But Alan lacked the drive to study
hard. He did not know why, but he had become an
average—actually, less-than-average—student at the
Naval Academy. At the Admiral Farragut Academy
he had done very well in his studies and had been
told that he had an IQ of 145. Now, at the Naval
Academy, he could not seem to translate this into
good grades. Classes at the Academy were rated on
a scale of 1 to 4, with 1 being very poor academi-
cally and 4 being outstanding. Alan and his
instructors were convinced that he was capable of
getting mainly 4s in his classes, but instead he was

averaging between a 2.5 and a 3.1. He was barely scraping by.

By October 1942, after nearly a year and a half at the Naval Academy, the situation was serious enough for Alan to be hauled before the institution's academic board. He was told that he ranked 676 out of 1,000 students and was asked whether he really wanted to become a naval officer. The board explained that if he did not improve his grades, he would be demoted and sent off to war as an enlisted sailor. Alan realized that this would mean the end of any hopes he had of becoming a naval pilot. Yet even this reality did not seem to motivate him to take his studies more seriously, and by Christmas 1942, he was well on his way to becoming an enlisted sailor swabbing the decks on a battleship somewhere in the Pacific Ocean.

Alan was glad to get away from Annapolis and the Naval Academy for the Christmas break. He decided to hop a ride on a navy cargo airplane to St. Louis, Missouri, where his sister Polly was a freshman at Principia College. From there he planned to take the train to Boston, Massachusetts, where his parents would pick him up and drive him home to East Derry for a traditional Christmas dinner. (Because he was in the military, Alan had a special train pass to travel. But wartime restrictions did not allow Polly to buy a train ticket home to New Hampshire, so she had to stay at college over the Christmas break.)

Alan promised himself that while he was away from the Naval Academy, he would not think about his poor grades or allow his father to talk about them.

Alan arrived at Principia College just in time to unload his rucksack, change into his dress uniform, and head out to the college Christmas dance. As tired as he was from traveling, Alan would never think of giving up an opportunity to socialize with a new group of young women. As soon as he entered the field house, which had been transformed into a dance hall for the event, Alan spotted a beautiful young woman with long, auburn hair and a tall, slim figure.

"Who's that?" he asked, nudging his sister.

Polly rolled her eyes. "Don't waste your time on her. That's Louise Brewer, and she has got a steady boyfriend."

"Well, I don't see him. Where is he?"

"He went home for Christmas. Set your sights a bit lower, Al," Polly replied dryly.

Alan grinned and strolled over to Louise, feeling confident in his navy blue uniform. "Hi, I'm Polly's brother Alan. Would you like to dance?" he asked.

Louise gave him a broad smile and nodded.

For the rest of the evening the two of them were inseparable, despite the fact that Louise often brought up her boyfriend, George, in the conversation. She also told Alan about her childhood. Her father was the head of maintenance at the DuPont family's compound, called Longwood Gardens, outside of Philadelphia. Mrs. DuPont had taken a special interest in Louise and her sister Adele and often brought them back stunning ball gowns from her trips to Europe. Louise's green eyes sparkled as she told Alan about the Christmas party the DuPonts held every year. The Brewers would sit on the balcony with Pierre and Alice DuPont as the Duponts gave gifts to hundreds of their workers and families. The entertainment at the party was always lavish, with live bands and a magnificent fireworks display to end the evening.

By the end of the night, Alan was totally smitten. He decided that he needed Louise Brewer to be his girlfriend, but to do this he would have to find a way to get her to drop George. Two nights later Alan and Louise were singing Christmas carols together, and as Alan looked into her green eyes, it confirmed everything he had already thought about her.

Two days before Christmas Alan said good-bye to Polly and Louise and took the train to Boston, where his parents were waiting to pick him up. Although he tried to think of other things to tell them on the drive back to East Derry, the topic of his conversation kept coming back to Louise Brewer.

As soon as he reached home, Alan wrote to Louise and invited her to his Ring Dance at the Naval Academy. Even though the dance wasn't until the end of the academic year, he desperately wanted her to agree to come to the event.

Christmas 1942 was more somber than past Christmases. Every serviceman and his family had the idea that this could be the last Christmas they spent together as a family, and Alan's family was no exception. In addition, the family received terrible news two days after Christmas. Alan's favorite cousin, Eric, had been killed in a crash during a pilot-training exercise. The entire Shepard family was devastated, and Alan immediately telegraphed the Naval Academy for permission to stay away longer to attend Eric's funeral in Massachusetts.

January 2, 1943, was a grim day as Alan wept at his cousin's graveside as Eric's body was buried. Following the funeral it was time to return to Annapolis and the Naval Academy. On the train ride back to the Academy Alan did some serious thinking. He pondered what he was doing at the Academy. He knew he had the IQ and the ability to be near the top of his class, yet he did not seem to be able to apply himself to his studies as he should. He thought about Eric, who had wanted so much to be a fighter pilot, and about Louise, who would surely find Alan more attractive if he was a naval aviator rather than a common sailor.

Somewhere between Massachusetts and Annapolis, Maryland, Alan made up his mind. It was time to get serious about his studies. If he tried really hard, he could pull himself out of his sinking grades, have the career he hoped for, and maybe even get the girl of his dreams.

When he arrived back at the Naval Academy, Alan added one more thing to his list: he wanted to graduate with a varsity letter, which meant that he was on the top team in a particular sport. The sport he set his sights on receiving his varsity letter in was the rowing eights.

Alan had been in the lower rowing teams since arriving in Annapolis, but most people did not give him any chance of gaining a letter in the rowing eights. It was obvious he did not have the right body shape to excel in the sport, obvious to everyone but Alan Shepard, that is. It was true that he was three or four inches shorter than anyone else on the varsity team and that he did not have long enough arms or the muscle strength to pull the oar in perfect unison, but Alan saw these as minor obstacles. With enough weight lifting and running, he was sure he could overcome them.

Soon Alan was spending much of his spare time in the gym lifting weights and doing countless push-ups in an attempt to build up his arm and upper-body strength. At dawn he would be up to practice with the team in the sixty-foot-long rowing shell. Alan would take his place in the rowing shell as the team rowed with all their might along the Severn River while their coach, Buck Walsh, who had won a gold medal in rowing at the 1920 Olympic Games, barked instructions to them through a bullhorn.

All of Alan's efforts in the gym paid off. His strength and determination caught Buck Walsh's attention, and Alan was made a permanent member of the senior rowing eights team.

Although Alan worked hard to get on the senior rowing team, he did not let his athletic training get in the way of his new focus on making good grades. By June 1943, Alan's combined sophomore/junior year, he had pulled his grades up enough to be on track to graduate from the Academy. This meant that he would be allowed to attend the Ring Dance.

The Ring Dance was a special event at which the juniors were given a Naval Academy ring, which they then dipped in a bowl containing water from the seven seas.

Alan had imagined Louise Brewer at his side as he dipped his ring into the bowl, but she had been reluctant to agree to make the trip to Annapolis for the event. Deep down Alan knew that if she did not come to Annapolis, it meant that he had probably lost her to George. But if Louise did come, it meant that she was interested in being his girlfriend. So Alan piled on the pressure, sending Louise a Valentine's Day card and a barrage of invitations to the Ring Dance. His persistence paid off, and finally Louise relented and agreed to be his date.

Louise came to Annapolis for a week, and she and Alan spent a wonderful time together, attending the senior graduation and sightseeing. Alan also took Louise boating on the Severn River and to many of his favorite local restaurants.

The Ring Dance was the pinnacle event of their week together, and it went off without a hitch. Louise wore a long, white gown to the dance, and Alan was the happiest man in attendance. By the end of the week, Alan was wondering whether he might be in love.

After Louise left Annapolis to return home, Alan did not have a lot of time to think about her. Within days of her departure, he found himself lugging his knapsack up the gangplank of the USS *Arkansas* for the three-week summer cruise that was the lot of every midshipman entering his senior year. The purpose of the cruise was to expose the cadets to the reality of shipboard life.

The *Arkansas* was an old World War I battleship the length of two football fields. Until he got his bearings, Alan often found himself lost in the maze of passageways in the bowels of the ship.

It was normal for the three-week cruise to head out to sea and up the East Coast to New York and Boston, but because German U-boats were now prowling off the East Coast of the United States, the *Arkansas* spent the duration of the cruise steaming up and down Chesapeake Bay. At that time of year the water in the bay was very warm, which in turn meant that the inside of the ship became very warm, and Alan passed many hot, sleepless nights in his bunk longing for the three-week cruise to come to an end, especially since he couldn't communicate with Louise until he was back on land.

The days aboard ship were not much better than the nights. Alan's days were spent undertaking menial tasks such as swabbing the wooden deck and polishing the brass fittings, along with learning how to navigate at sea using a compass, a sextant, and the stars.

All in all, like the other midshipmen aboard, Alan could hardly wait to get ashore as the *Arkansas* tied up alongside the dock at the end of the three-week cruise. His time aboard the USS *Arkansas* had shown him two things: First, he was not built to be a sailor and so needed to aggressively pursue his love of flying. And second, he missed Louise Brewer terribly.

When he got back to the Naval Academy, Alan called Louise and professed his love to her. Louise was shocked. "Alan," she replied, "I think a lot of you, but as I said once before, I haven't known you very long. And," she added pointedly, "I've known George for nine years."

A lesser man might have taken this as a gentle letdown, but not Alan Shepard. He was determined to win Louise over, but it was not until October that he had the chance to see her again. Things went well, and at the end of their week together, Louise confessed that she felt very confused about whom she really loved. But as time went on, she became convinced that Alan was the man for her. Alan, of course, was delighted by this piece of news.

Things during Alan's last year as a midshipman at the Academy continued to go his way. He remained a member of the senior rowing eights team, his grades went up to a respectable level, and the war raged on in Europe and the Pacific, making it probable that he would get a chance to fight.

As he neared graduation, Alan wrote to his grandmother Shepard back in East Derry. "I could never have been happier in any other place. It has put me on my two feet, entirely independent, and has broadened my outlook and matured me much more evenly than any other college or university could have done in three years," he wrote.

Soon afterward, Alan, a confident twenty-year-old, graduated from the U.S. Naval Academy in Annapolis, Maryland. His parents and Louise were by his side for the graduation ceremony. The inscription in the Academy's yearbook about Alan read, "With his personality and ability, he should go far." Neither Alan nor anyone else in his graduating class had any idea just how far, or how fast, he was destined to go.

Chapter 5

Into Battle

Naval policy did not allow a junior officer to begin flight training until he had served one year aboard a ship. So Alan and his friend and former Naval Academy roommate, Bob Williams, strode across the San Francisco Navy Yard on the way to find their names on the roster of men being shipped out on various military-transport ships to their first assignments. Alan had been assigned as a junior officer on the destroyer USS *Cogswell,* and Bob was assigned to the light cruiser USS *Cleveland.* To the two former roommates' mutual disappointment, they also had been assigned to travel on different transport ships. Alan would be traveling aboard the USAT *Willard A. Holbrook.*

Alan had never heard of the *Willard A. Holbrook,* and when he asked a nearby officer about the ship, the officer chuckled. "You've got yourself a real old rust bucket there!" he said.

It was not what Alan wanted to hear. But the news got worse. Alan soon learned that the *Willard A. Holbrook* was a twenty-four-year-old vessel that had been requisitioned by the military to carry troops around the Pacific Islands. The ship was originally built as a passenger liner but had spent most of her life hauling jute, spices, and coconuts around the Pacific. Apparently much of that cargo often rotted in the vessel's hold. In fact, the ship still smelled so bad from all this spoiled cargo that it had been nicknamed the "Stinkin' Old Holbrook."

In late August 1944, as Alan climbed the gangway and boarded the *Willard A. Holbrook,* his nose quickly told him the ship's nickname was not an exaggeration. A rotting smell had seeped into every nook and cranny of the vessel. Not only that, the ship was every bit the rust bucket Alan had been told she was. In fact, the ship was even more decrepit than Alan had imagined she would be, and her hull and superstructure were more rusted than any ship he had ever seen.

As the mooring lines that held the transport ship to the dock were let go, Alan joined the other military personnel being transported aboard her at the rail to wave good-bye to the crowd assembled on the dock. Among them Alan spotted Louise Brewer, who had secretly agreed to marry him when the war was over.

The *Willard A. Holbrook* steamed out of San Francisco Bay and headed southwest at a rate of eighteen knots. Its first stop would be the island of Biak, off the coast of New Guinea, which had recently been captured from the Japanese in a fierce battle and now served as an Allied staging area. The trip to Biak was long and torturous, and Alan shared a tiny cabin with four other men. Sometimes it was so hot in the bowels of the ship that they all preferred to go up and sleep on deck in the open with only a sheet over them. During the day, everyone aboard kept a nervous lookout for Japanese submarines. Then one dark night the loudspeaker blared the dreaded words "Submarine to port side. Extinguish all lights and remain in complete silence." Alan would have liked to have heard the loudspeaker announce, "Man battle stations," but since there were no battle stations on the old ship, everyone aboard waited anxiously right where he was.

Alan and several of the ship's officers peered into the dark water off the port side of the vessel. As they stared, they saw a curved black shape emerge from the water. Alan gulped. The *Willard A. Holbrook* was a sitting duck. Suddenly a spout of water shot up into the air, and everyone breathed a sigh of relief. It wasn't a Japanese submarine after all, but a surfacing whale. Soon the ship was again under way at full steam.

Finally, six weeks after setting out from San Francisco, the ship reached Biak, a tiny volcanic island. When Alan went ashore, he caught his first glimpse of the brutality of war. The corpses of dead Japanese soldiers, some burned, others beheaded, littered the previously picturesque tropical island, a reminder of the bitter battle that had been waged to capture the island. For once, the stench of the rotting corpses made the *Willard A. Holbrook* smell pleasant by comparison.

On its second afternoon in port at Biak, the *Willard A. Holbrook* was hit, not by a Japanese torpedo but by a U.S. Navy ship. The second ship was maneuvering into the narrow harbor when the pilot miscalculated and sent the ship careening toward the *Holbrook*. From shore, where he sat with some buddies, Alan watched the whole incident, mesmerized by the sight and sound of one metal hull slamming into another.

The damage to the *Holbrook* was repairable, but it meant that the ship would have to spend longer in port while the repairs were made. Alan quickly decided what to do with this spare time. He befriended several B-25 bomber pilots and wangled a seat on a practice bombing run. Alan was allowed to ride along with the nose gunner, situated in a Plexiglas bubble at the front of the bomber, right beneath the pilot. The B-25 made several bombing runs at an abandoned ship used for target practice. On one of these bombing runs, the nose gunner let Alan take control of the machine gun and blast away at the abandoned ship. It was an exhilarating experience for Alan as he felt the gun vibrate in his hand when he pulled the trigger and saw a stream of bullets smashing into the side of the old ship.

Finally it was time to return to Biak, and the pilot banked the bomber in a steep turn as he set course for the island. As the plane banked around, the pilot spotted several Japanese warships in the distance. He headed the airplane toward them, and as they closed in on the ships, the gunner took the machine-gun controls from Alan and began strafing the Japanese ships with bullets.

It was the only aerial combat Alan would experience during the war, but what he had experienced excited him. It also made the thought of having to spend the next year on a ship as a junior officer seem tedious. Alan believed he was made to fly, not to sail the seas.

Back on the ground at Biak, repairs to the *Willard A. Holbrook's* damaged hull were finally completed, and Alan climbed back aboard the old rust bucket. The destination this time was Ulithi Atoll in the Western Caroline Islands, which American troops had recently captured from the Japanese and which was now being used as a navy base and staging area. At Ulithi, Alan would finally link up with the USS *Cogswell.*

When Alan finally laid eyes on the *Cogswell* on October 30, 1944, he was shocked. The destroyer was only a year old, but as the veteran of several sea battles in and around the Philippine Islands, Indonesia, and New Guinea, her hull was rusted and pockmarked with bullet holes from Japanese aircraft. Still, after so many weeks on the "Stinkin' Old Holbrook," transferring to a battle-scarred destroyer was a delight for Alan as he packed his few belongings into a rucksack and prepared to join his new ship.

From the moment he climbed the gangplank to the 2000-ton *Cogswell,* Alan felt like he was really a part of the war. The destroyer was armed with ten 21-inch torpedo tubes, five 5-inch guns, six depth-charge projectors, and two depth- charge tracks and could cruise at a speed of thirty-five knots. The ship's mission was to find and destroy Japanese submarines and provide support to other ships and ground troops.

On November 1, the *Cogswell,* with Alan Shepard aboard as the most junior of junior officers, set sail from Ulithi. Finally Alan was going to see some real fighting action. His first assignment aboard ship was to man the vessel's internal telephone switchboard. But Alan considered being a switchboard operator easy work, and he put in a request to be transferred to the gunnery division, where he would be on deck and in the middle of all the action.

Two nights after leaving port, the USS *Cogswell* and a cruiser, the USS *Reno,* were steaming along together off the San Bernardino Strait in the Philippines when an enormous explosion rocked the *Cogswell.* Alan and everyone else aboard felt the blast and soon realized what had happened. The USS *Reno* had been hit by a torpedo from a Japanese submarine and was sinking fast. Whistles and horns blew as the sailors on the *Cogswell* manned their battle stations while Alan sat at the switchboard below, wondering what was happening on deck. Finally he learned that the *Reno* was on fire, listing badly, and in danger of sinking. The vessel's captain had issued the order to abandon ship.

For the next several hours, the sailors aboard the *Cogswell* were kept busy rescuing members of the *Reno*'s crew from the oil-slicked ocean, all the while hoping a torpedo would not hit their ship as well. No torpedo hit the *Cogswell*, and when the rescue was over, 172 sailors from the *Reno* had been saved, while 46 had lost their lives in the attack. Though badly damaged, the USS *Reno* did not sink. She sat low in the water with only a few feet of freeboard keeping her afloat, while oil continued to pour from her port side. The torpedo and depth charges aboard the waterlogged *Reno* were jettisoned to lighten her load, and then the *Cogswell* took the vessel in tow. The ships headed back to Ulithi, where temporary repairs could be made to the *Reno.*

Along the way on the trip back, the *Cogswell* had to fend off Japanese suicide pilots who tried to fly their small fighter planes into the ship in order to destroy it. These pilots were called kamikazes, and it took lightning-fast reflexes to shoot them down before they could inflict their damage on a ship.

The USS *Cogswell* towed the *Reno* within sight of Ulithi Atoll, only to be confronted with a radio message that Japanese minisubmarines had been observed in the area. The crews of the ships at the atoll were to be on high alert for an attack. In the early hours of the morning, a nearby navy tanker was hit, and an ensuing fireball lit up the sky. The entire crew of the tanker was killed in the attack, and all Alan and his crewmates could do was watch the fiery inferno and pray that their ship would not be torpedoed next.

Again no torpedo hit the *Cogswell,* and at dawn the ship was allowed to pass through a channel in the reef and pull the USS *Reno* into the relatively safe refuge of Ulithi's lagoon. For their efforts, the crew of the USS *Cogswell* was awarded a unit citation for rescuing the *Reno*'s crew and escorting the waterlogged vessel safely back to port.

Alan had had his first taste of combat, and he was ready for more. A few days later the *Cogswell* once again set out to join the battle to free the small islands of the western Pacific from their Japanese invaders.

As it happened, their next battle was not with the Japanese but with the forces of nature. December was typhoon season in the western Pacific Ocean, and the crew of the *Cogswell* soon learned just how powerful a typhoon could be. Caught off guard by the storm, the *Cogswell* endured 120-mile-an-hour winds as it was tossed about like a toy. The ship rode to the crest of thirty-foot-high waves and then would surf down into the troughs, slamming her hull hard as it bottomed out. For two days most of the ship's crew were strapped into their bunks; meals were suspended, and only a few essential sailors were allowed above deck.

When the typhoon finally abated, Alan learned that several of his crewmates had been washed overboard. As well, three other U.S. warships caught in the storm had capsized. The *Cogswell* joined in the search for survivors of these ships, pulling a number of men aboard from shark-infested waters. Alan recognized some of the survivors from his graduating class at the Naval Academy. In all, 790 American sailors lost their lives as a result of the typhoon.

On Christmas Eve 1944, the *Cogswell* delivered the survivors who had been rescued back to Ulithi. Safely at anchor in the atoll's lagoon, the ship's crew enjoyed a hearty Christmas dinner of turkey with all the trimmings and picked up their mail.

This was supposed to be a happy time, but sadly for Alan, the long-awaited mail brought bad news from home. His beloved grandmother Nanzie Shepard had fallen in the snow three weeks before and died in the hospital. Alan was devastated. So many of his happy childhood memories revolved around Grandma Nanzie and her efforts to make him a strong, self-reliant boy. Now, he knew, he would never see her again.

The only spark of good news was that the USS *Cogswell* was slated for a general overhaul in California in two months, and Alan and his crewmates would get four weeks' liberty leave in the United States!

Alan knew just what he wanted to do with his leave: he wanted to marry Louise and enjoy a brief honeymoon. He wrote to Louise suggesting the idea, though he knew he would not get a reply until he reached the West Coast of the United States.

The voyage home across the Pacific Ocean was uneventful, and in early February 1945, Alan flew from Long Beach, California, to Louise's home in

Pennsylvania to make last-minute plans to marry her. Among these plans was the task of asking Mr. Brewer for the hand of his daughter in marriage. It was a tense moment. The Brewers were obviously shocked. They had no idea that Alan and Louise were secretly engaged, and now Alan was standing in their living room, asking if they could arrange a marriage to their daughter in a week.

Reluctantly the Brewers agreed to the idea, and a hurried wedding was planned. The minister from St. Stephen's Lutheran Church in Wilmington, Delaware, did not seem surprised about the haste of the wedding. So many young men and women were getting married on leave from the army and navy. Many of them barely knew each other, but what they did know was that they were fighting in a war and they wanted something "normal" to cling to as they faced battle.

The wedding was held on March 3, 1945. Alan wore his dress uniform, as did his father who served as the best man. Louise had managed to find a beautiful white satin gown, and Alan thought she looked every inch a lady. It had been less than two and a half years since he'd first laid eyes on Louise at Polly's college Christmas ball, and now they were standing together, husband and wife, about to embark on life together.

Their honeymoon in the White Mountains of New Hampshire was short and poignant, since Alan had to return to the war in the Pacific. Louise decided to move to San Francisco to be nearer to him and to gain the support of other military wives.

The couple flew back across the country and found Louise an apartment to share in San Francisco.

On April 5, 1945, the refurbished USS *Cogswell* once again set sail for battle. Alan stood on deck and watched as his new wife waved a brave good-bye. It was the hardest good-bye he had ever faced.

The *Cogswell* put in at Pearl Harbor, Hawaii, where Alan received word that he had been reassigned from his switchboard duties to something much more to his liking—a deck officer overseeing the 20-millimeter and 40-millimeter antiaircraft guns mounted on the ship's bow. With the Japanese using more and more kamikaze attacks against American ships, the antiaircraft guns were an important line of defense.

In the waters off the Hawaiian coast, the *Cogswell* conducted maneuvers for a week so that the crew could get used to their new roles before the ship was thrust back into the thick of the battle. Alan also used this time in Hawaii to apply for navy flight school. He still had four months to go before he reached his one-year mark at sea, but he did not want to spend one day longer aboard ship than he had to.

"One of these days," he told a friend who stood watch with him one night, "if I don't get killed, I am going to learn to fly."

Soon after this, the war entered a new phase. President Franklin Roosevelt died, and four weeks later the Germans surrendered. To the people back home in the United States, this was a good thing, but to Alan Shepard and the other men fighting the

Japanese in the Pacific, it was a bad thing. The Japanese were now the only country at war with the Allies, and as they became more desperate, they carried out more and more lethal suicide missions.

When the *Cogswell* finally made it back to the western Pacific, it was put to work on picket duty off the coast of Okinawa. Two months before, the Marines had begun the invasion of the island of Okinawa (located 340 miles south of Japan), where one hundred thousand Japanese soldiers were purportedly entrenched. To stop the Japanese from reinforcing their troops, the island was ringed with naval vessels. The ships lined up side by side in a row, like the pickets of a fence; hence, manning the line became known as picket duty. In all, more than thirteen hundred navy ships participated in the picket.

Picket duty was no easy task. The desperate Japanese sent wave after wave of kamikaze planes at the ships, hoping to disrupt the line. During its time on the picket line, the *Cogswell* saw its share of action. Alan spent hours, night and day, scanning the sky for incoming Japanese aircraft. When they were spotted, a tremendous thundering would break loose as the antiaircraft guns on the *Cogswell* and the vessels around her opened fire. Although the *Cogswell* was not hit directly by a kamikaze airplane, plenty of other ships were. The USS *Porter,* which held the line beside the *Cogswell,* was hit by a kamikaze plane and sank. All of the sailors aboard her were rescued, but other sailors were not so fortunate when their ships were hit and sunk.

Finally, in July, the battle for Okinawa was over, but not before kamikaze attacks had damaged 198 warships, sinking 17 of them and killing more than three thousand sailors.

Following picket duty off Okinawa, the USS *Cogswell* was stationed off the coast of Japan with orders to bomb the coastline. But still the Japanese refused to admit defeat. Then on August 6, 1945, the United States dropped an atomic bomb on the Japanese city of Hiroshima, the first atomic bomb ever to be used in warfare. Eighty thousand people were killed instantly in the blast, and 70 percent of the buildings in the city were destroyed. Still the Japanese would not surrender. Three days later another atomic bomb was dropped, this time on the city of Nagasaki. Nagasaki was located only one hundred miles from the *Cogswell*'s position off the coast, and the massive explosion jolted the whole ship. Finally the Japanese had had enough and surrendered. On August 15, 1945, a cease-fire order was issued to all Allied ships and troops.

Twelve days later, the USS *Cogswell* was given the honor of being the first navy ship to steam into Tokyo Bay, leading a proud but battered flotilla of Allied warships. In Tokyo Bay, the Japanese signed formal surrender papers aboard the battleship USS *Missouri* on September 2. World War II was officially over.

Although Alan never got to fly during the war, he had survived when many of his counterparts had not. He knew he was blessed to be alive, and as it happened, he was about to get wonderful news.

The fighting in the Pacific and in Europe had proved one thing: airplanes were now an integral part of modern warfare. As a result, the U.S. government had decided to put money and time into developing the best air force in the world, an air force that would be so strong that other countries would not want to pit themselves against it. To do this, the U.S. Air Force recruited the best and bravest of the World War II fighters to train as pilots to fly the most advanced fighter airplanes ever built.

In mid-September 1945, at the end of his year as an officer at sea and while still aboard the USS *Cogswell*, Alan received word that he had been accepted by the navy for flight training. He whooped with joy when he received the news. It wasn't too late for him, after all. His dream to fly was about to come true.

Chapter 6

Zoom Town

Corpus Christi—Alan and Louise Shepard peered down at the map spread out between them.

"It's almost in Mexico," Louise said.

"Yep," Alan agreed. "About one hundred fifty miles from the border. I hear there was nothing down there but cattle ranches and oil wells until the navy started its air-training facility five years ago."

"Texas is a long way from home," Louise said. "But then, as long as we're together, we can make a home anywhere. We've been married eight months already, and this will be the first time we get to live together."

Alan smiled at his wife and reached for her hand. It sure was nice, he thought, to have someone to travel through life with.

A week later Alan and Louise loaded up their car and set out for Corpus Christi. They followed the route they had plotted on the map: from San Francisco south, and then east across the deserts of Arizona, New Mexico, and West Texas, through San Antonio and finally on to Corpus Christi, nestled on the shore of the Gulf of Mexico.

Even though it was November, late fall in the north, the air in Corpus Christi was warm and humid. Date palms and oleander trees lined the streets as Alan and Louise drove to the naval air station. Commissioned in 1941 to train pilots for World War II, the Corpus Christi Naval Air Station, sprawled over twenty thousand acres of land, was the largest flight-training center in the world. In the four years since the place opened, thirty thousand pilots had gone through its training programs.

As they approached the air station, Alan stared out the open car window. To his surprise he could not see a single aircraft anywhere. *What kind of a flight school doesn't have airplanes?* he wondered.

The mystery was soon unraveled when Alan and Louise arrived at the naval air station. A hurricane had just blown through the area, and all of the aircraft stationed at the base had been flown north to Dallas, Texas, to avoid being damaged by the storm. As it was, a number of the base's 997 hangars had been damaged by the high winds.

Alan and Louise rented a two-story apartment on Ocean Drive, a perfect location situated by the ocean and halfway between the air station and the town of Corpus Christi. They bought a few basic pieces of furniture and moved in. Soon they were making preparations for their first Thanksgiving meal together.

Just before the Thanksgiving holiday, repairs to the hurricane-damaged hangars were finally completed, and airplanes began flying back into the air station. Soon all manner of aircraft—biplanes, cargo planes, seaplanes, tanker planes, and helicopters, some powered by single props, others by twin props—began passing overhead like a swarm of locusts on their way to the air station. Alan could clearly see why Corpus Christi had been dubbed "Zoom Town." As the swarm of planes passed over him, Alan knew that there was no other place in the world he would rather be at that moment, despite the stifling heat of Corpus Christi.

Alan and Louise enjoyed Thanksgiving dinner together, and the following day, November 26, 1945, Alan donned his new uniform and drove to the Corpus Christi Naval Air Station to begin his flight training.

While Alan was busy studying, Louise stayed home, arranging the apartment, doing needlepoint, participating in the young-wives' group at the local Christian Science Church, and taking long walks through town. At night she would often tell Alan things she had learned about Corpus Christi from her walks. For example, she learned that the town began in 1839 when Colonel Henry Lawrence Kinney established a trading post there to sell supplies to a Mexican revolutionary army that was camped about twenty-five miles to the west.

Alan was glad to see that his wife was keeping busy, though he knew she had been worrying about him from the time he started his training. All of the wives were worried about their husbands, and with good cause. Alan had been in the flight-training program only two months when he heard the sound of the buzzer resonate across the base. The purpose of the buzzer was to signal that there had been a crash, and when he heard it, Alan spun around just in time to see a maelstrom of fiery pieces of twisted metal falling into the Gulf of Mexico just beyond the air station.

At first the sight of the crash took him back to his days aboard the USS *Cogswell* where they would shoot down Japanese kamikaze airplanes that crashed into the ocean in fireballs. But this time it was not Japanese aircraft that had been shot down. Instead, two seaplanes, one taking off and the other coming in to land at the air station, had crashed into each other about two hundred feet up. Twenty-two trainees lost their lives in the accident, and five survived, though they were severely wounded. Alan knew it could have been him aboard one of those airplanes. His life, and the lives of his fellow flight trainees hung in a perilous balance.

Other accidents followed. The flight-training officers said that it was bound to happen with three hundred airplanes in the air at the same time. Sometimes the planes were forced to share the same runway, with planes taking off on the right side while others landed on the left side. In just one year there were 5,532 accidents that killed ninety-one men.

Alan's first month of training was spent in the classroom, studying physics, astronomy, celestial navigation, and basic mechanics. It was a frustrating time for him. He wanted to be in the air flying, not stuck in the tedious routine of classroom study. To make matters worse, with so many trainees at the air station and only so many training aircraft available, trainees had to take their place in line waiting for their chance to finally climb into an airplane cockpit and take to the skies. Each afternoon the trainees would traipse out to one of the hangars to see whether their names appeared on the day's flight list written up on a chalkboard. Finally, on January 10, 1946, Alan spotted his name on the day's list. At last he was headed aloft.

Alan strode confidently across the tarmac to plane 64, a single-engine, two-seater Stearman N2S biplane. The plane was painted bright yellow, as were all the training planes, and as a result the Stearman biplanes had the nickname "Yellow Peril." Waiting beside this particular Yellow Peril was Ensign J. C. Pennock, Alan's flight instructor.

Alan climbed into the front cockpit of the Stearman biplane, and Ensign Pennock took his place in the cockpit behind. A rubber tube stretched between the two cockpits through which the instructor could bark instructions to his student. Ensign Pennock cranked the Yellow Peril's engine and taxied the plane out to the runway, where they waited in line for their turn to take off. Soon they were airborne, and Alan could feel the exhilarating slap of the air against his face. As they circled out over the Gulf of Mexico, Ensign Pennock instructed Alan to lightly place his hands on the control stick and his toes on the rudder pedals. Alan did as he was told, and his instructor pointed out that this was to get him oriented to the movement of the stick and rudder pedals as the instructor flew the plane from the rear cockpit. Finally, after a few flights like this, Alan would take the controls and maneuver the aircraft in flight.

Soon the thirty-minute circuit out across the Gulf of Mexico was over, and Ensign Pennock guided the plane back to a soft landing at the air station. Alan could hardly wait for his next flight.

During the next several flights, Ensign Pennock instructed Alan in how to taxi the biplane on the ground, adjust the fuel mixture for takeoff, adjust the throttle to full, guide the plane down the runway, and then slowly pull back on the control stick and guide the aircraft into the air when it had picked up enough speed.

On one of their flights, with Alan at the controls, the Yellow Peril's engine began to sputter and almost cut out. Ensign Pennock grabbed the plane's controls from Alan and nursed the plane back to the air station before the engine cut out completely and they were forced to make a crash landing. They managed to arrive back on the runway safely, but the incident sapped some of Alan's usual confidence, and he found himself becoming more hesitant at the controls.

Nonetheless, his flight instructor decided that Alan was ready for his first solo flight. Alan climbed nervously into the Yellow Peril's cockpit, strapped himself in, and cranked up the engine. He then proceeded to taxi out to the runway, though in his nervous state he concentrated so much on his own airplane that he forgot to look out for other planes taxiing on the ground. However, he did not hit any other aircraft and managed to get the Stearman into the air, though not as smoothly as his instructor had shown him. Alan flew the plane out over the Gulf of Mexico before circling back to the air station to land. Again, his approach and landing were not as smooth as Ensign Pennock had demonstrated. Still, Alan was elated. He had finally flown an airplane solo. He could hardly wait to get home to tell Louise about the experience.

More solo flights followed, until it was time for his first evaluation, or "check flight," as it was called. For this flight Ensign Pennock once again climbed into the rear cockpit and proceeded to grade Alan's pilot performance as he took off, flew the plane in a circuit over the Gulf of Mexico, and then landed.

Although Alan felt that it wasn't his best flying performance, he was shocked when he saw the results of his check flight. The instructor noted that Alan had waited too long to lift into the air on take-off, that he had swerved when taxiing, and that once airborne, he had allowed the plane to "skid."

The official record showed that Alan received one "good" grade, seventeen "satisfactory" grades, and five "borderline" grades for his check flight. Borderline was as low as a trainee could go before receiving an "unsatisfactory" grade. And getting an unsatisfactory led to receiving a "down check," which meant the trainee pilot was grounded and would most likely be dismissed from the flight-training program.

Alan knew that his instructor had gone easy on him. He was frustrated with himself. He had been around airplanes for so long that he assumed he would be a natural, quick-learning student of flight. That night he went home to Louise feeling dejected and unsure of his future. What would he do if he was down-checked and removed from the program?

Louise gave Alan her usual steadying advice: "Work harder, don't be overconfident, do exactly what the instructor says instead of trying to do it your own way, and don't give up."

It was at moments like this that Alan knew he had married the right woman. He did tend to be overconfident and to approach things like a race-horse at full gallop, often ignoring instruction in his quest to do things his way. At times like that, Louise was the slow, quiet influence that reined him in and refocused him on his goals.

Still, satisfying Ensign Pennock and the other flight instructors was no easy task, and Alan continued to get negative comments on his evaluations. "Very unsteady and erratic...didn't think," one instructor scribbled on his evaluation. And "GOING

IN THE WRONG DIRECTION," another instructor scrawled.

Despite all his effort, by June 1946, six months into his flight training, Alan's name had been placed on the short list of want-to-be-pilots who would probably be reassigned back to the regular navy. His performance, with the exception of night flying, was well below average, and better men were waiting in line to take his place. This situation finally prompted Alan to take severe action. He felt that the root of his flying problems lay in his lack of solo flying time, where he could work out for himself the kinks in his approach to flying. In fact, the program was so crowded that during his six months of flight training he had spent less than a hundred hours in the cockpit of an airplane, flying it. Alan knew that he needed more practice, and he was not going to get it with the navy. He decided to do something about it. He arranged to take private flying lessons.

Of course, since the navy frowned upon this, Alan had to secretly arrange for the lessons at a nearby airfield. As he took the lessons, spending more and more time in the air flying, he worked hard to do everything that his instructor told him to do. His effort paid off. Within three months Alan had earned his private pilot's license and had a renewed commitment to do the very best he could in his naval flight-training program. Just as he had at the Naval Academy in Annapolis, Alan pulled himself out of his complacency and back on to the road to distinguishing himself among his fellow officers. As he did so, he wondered if he didn't need the experience of sinking so low before he really started to apply himself to the task at hand and pop up to the top.

Now every morning before he set out for the naval air station, Alan looked in the mirror and said to himself, "You know something? You didn't do as good a job yesterday as you should have. You goofed off a little bit." And then he would resolve to do better that day.

He also had one more reason other than personal pride to succeed in his flight training. Louise was expecting a baby, due in July 1947, and Alan wanted his career to be moving forward by then.

Alan's perseverance paid off. His grades steadily rose, and before he knew it, it was time for him to transfer to the Pensacola Naval Air Station in Florida to complete his flight training. This was the demanding final phase of training, during which he was required to take off and land an airplane six times on the deck of an aircraft carrier cruising in the Gulf of Mexico.

At the Pensacola Naval Air Station, Alan learned all he could from the instructors and other pilots before setting sail aboard the aircraft carrier USS *Saipan.* Aboard the carrier with him was Alan's father, for whom Alan had managed to secure a place on the voyage. Bart Shepard showed up dressed in full military uniform, camera in hand, ready to capture on film his son qualifying as a navy pilot.

On their second day at sea, Alan and a group of other trainee pilots prepared for their series of take-offs and landings on the USS *Saipan*. Alan would be flying an SNJ Texan, a single-wing training aircraft propelled by a powerful Pratt and Whitney engine. Landing an airplane on the deck of an aircraft carrier was difficult enough in calm conditions, but as Alan climbed into the cockpit of the Texan, a stiff wind was blowing, which would make his task, particularly landing, more difficult.

Before long Alan was airborne. He circled out over the Gulf of Mexico from the *Saipan*'s deck, taking his place in line to make his approach and landing back on the ship. As he circled, Alan watched the two airplanes in front of him as they made their approach and landing attempts. To his dismay, both of these landing attempts were aborted at the last minute because the pilots had been unable to line up their airplanes properly with the flight deck.

Finally it was Alan's turn to land. He approached the ship in the prescribed manner, flying ahead of the vessel and then making a series of U-turns that put him behind the *Saipan*. He then began a slow descent toward the ship, all the while looking out for the LSO (landing signal officer). The LSO was perched right at the end of the flight deck. His job, using paddles, was to signal to the landing pilot and guide him down to the deck to land.

Soon Alan spotted the LSO. He throttled back the aircraft until it was just above stall speed.

Slowly the Texan airplane approached the landing deck. Then a gust of wind blew. The Texan rocked from side to side, and Alan noticed the LSO tilt one of his signal paddles, indicating that Alan was off course and needed to realign the plane. Alan quickly got his bearings and adjusted his course. He was now again lined up properly, and the LSO signaled him so. Alan cautiously approached the flight deck, fretting that he might overfly the ship. At that moment he saw the LSO drop down his signal paddles. It was time to cut power. Alan reached over and pulled the throttle right back while momentarily dropping the airplane's nose and then pulling it up. As he did so, he felt the thud of the Texan's wheels on the deck of the *Saipan*. He was down!

The plane bounced forward on the deck, and then the tailhook caught one of the arresting wires that ran across the flight deck. The wire cable stretched for a moment and then became rigid, pulling the Texan to a complete halt and flinging Alan forward against his harness. He had done it! He had landed safely on the deck of an aircraft carrier. Now all that he needed was to do it five more times and he would be qualified to serve as a navy pilot.

When Alan emerged from the cockpit of the SNJ Texan, his father was there with the camera to snap a shot of his son and tell him about the great pictures he had taken of Alan's landing.

Five more near-perfect landings followed for Alan, and when it was all over, he stood at attention on the deck of the USS *Saipan*. Bart Shepard was then given the honor of pinning the naval aviator's wings and anchor onto his son's uniform. Alan did not need a camera to keep a mental snapshot of that proud moment in his mind for the rest of his life.

Chapter 7

Wingman

F ive days after qualifying and now a navy pilot, Alan stood staring at a piece of paper. On it were typed the letters *VF*, navy lingo for fighter squadron. Alan let out a whoop of joy. He had been assigned to learn to fly single-engine fighter planes, the most elite and dangerous job in the navy, rather than learn to fly the navy's big and lumbering transport aircraft. To be assigned to a fighter squadron was an honor for any twenty-three-year-old, and Alan considered himself blessed to be so assigned, given his mixed grades early on in the program back at the Corpus Christi Naval Air Station.

Alan and Louise had one week to pack up their belongings and report to Cecil Field in Jacksonville, Florida. They made it there a day ahead of schedule, and Alan eagerly went to inspect his new airfield and walk around some of the airplanes he would be piloting. He was especially interested in learning to fly the F4U Corsair, a notoriously difficult plane to fly but whose maneuverability in the air and sheer speed had helped to turn the tide of World War II in favor of the Allies in the Pacific theater of operations. Alan admired the sleek but ungainly-looking aircraft. The plane was powered by a massive 2,000-horsepower, 18-cylinder Pratt and Whitney engine that spun a 4-bladed, 13-foot-diameter propeller, which in turn allowed the plane to travel at over four hundred miles per hour in the air. The aircraft had a long nose, with the cockpit located behind the V-shaped gull wings. While it was fast and agile once airborne, the F4U Corsair's long nose greatly obscured a pilot's forward vision during landings and takeoffs and while taxiing on the ground. Because of its long nose, the Corsair was often referred to by the nickname "Hog."

In the next three months Alan tested himself against the Corsair, learning the aircraft's quirks and how to control the plane in the air. The Corsair had a tendency, because of its powerful engine, to pull to the left during takeoff. To combat this tendency, a pilot needed to almost stand on the right rudder pedal. The engine could also stall at low speed, and when it did, the Corsair would flip to the right before a pilot had a chance to correct. This tendency often ended in the plane's crashing into the ground in a fireball. But Alan learned how to deal with the Corsair's anomalies, and soon he was

zooming along at the airplane's top speed. He liked
nothing better when flying at this speed than to
"crack the whip." This meant pulling back on the
control stick so that the Corsair climbed quickly,
throwing Alan back into his seat with a force seven
times that of gravity. Then Alan would rapidly jerk
the control stick forward, altering the plane's pitch
in the air and creating an air pocket behind the
wings. The air that rushed in to fill this air pocket
would let out a loud clap that sounded like the
crack of a whip.

The long hours Alan put in learning to master
the Corsair in the air were lonely hours for Louise,
who was battling morning sickness from her preg-
nancy. In July Louise headed to Pennsylvania to stay
with her parents and prepare for the baby's arrival.

With his fighter training behind him, Alan
moved on to Norfolk, Virginia, the home of Navy
Fighter Squadron VF-42. The squadron was attached
to the aircraft carrier USS *Franklin D. Roosevelt*, or
the *FDR*, as most people called it. The 45,000-ton,
968-foot-long *FDR* had been launched April 29,
1945, at the New York Naval Shipyard. It was originally christened the USS *Coral Sea*, but following
the death of President Roosevelt on May 8, 1945,
the vessel had been renamed in his honor.

When Alan arrived at the naval base at Norfolk,
the *FDR* was in dry dock undergoing a major overhaul. This gave Alan the opportunity to settle into
his new responsibilities with the fighter squadron
while still on land. As he did so, his flying abilities
came to the attention of his squadron commander,

James L. "Doc" Abbot. Doc Abbot was so impressed with Alan that from among the thirty-six men who made up the squadron, he chose Alan to be his wingman.

Being chosen to be wingman was the ultimate vote of confidence of one pilot in another. A wingman would fly slightly behind his partner where he would act as helper and defender. The two pilots would stay in close radio contact, and if any enemy aircraft were about to attack his partner, the wingman would point them out and then come to his partner's aid in the fight. The wingman also made sure that no airplanes attacked his partner from behind.

In July 1947, as he continued his fighter training, Alan received word that Louise had given birth to their first child, a daughter, whom they named Laura. As soon as he could get away, Alan headed to Pennsylvania to visit his wife and new daughter. During the visit, as Alan and Louise talked, they realized that Louise would be happier staying on with her parents, at least until the baby was a few months old.

After the visit, Alan returned to his fighter-pilot duties with the navy. Eventually, several months after Laura's birth, Louise moved to Norfolk, and the Shepard family was reunited in one spot but not for long. In early 1948 the overhaul on the FDR was complete, and the vessel was ready for its "shakedown" voyage, the opportunity for the ship and crew to mesh into one unit and iron out any mechanical or procedural problems that might emerge.

Alan stood on deck as the massive *FDR* steamed away from Norfolk and then headed south toward the Caribbean Sea. The first stop was Guantanamo Bay, Cuba. Following the stop at Guantanamo Bay, the *FDR* sailed southwest toward Jamaica. It was now time to see what the new members of Fighter Squadron VF-42 were made of.

Alan was eager to try his hand at landing the Corsair on the deck of the aircraft carrier; he got his chance soon enough. Given the airplane's poor forward visibility during landing and takeoff, this was no easy task, but Alan soon mastered the art. Over and over again he practiced taking off and landing until he felt confident he could do it with his eyes shut or at least in the dark.

Always up for the next challenge, Alan asked his commander, Doc Abbot, if he could attempt a night landing, even though this was not standard practice for new pilots, or "nuggets," as they were called. Still, Alan would not take no for an answer, and eventually he wore Doc Abbot down. Doc Abbot agreed to let Alan attempt a night landing, though not before he pointed out a few special characteristics of the Corsair that made it particularly dangerous to land on an aircraft carrier at night. The biggest problem, again, was poor forward visibility from the cockpit during landing. Visibility was obscured even further by darkness. Alan likened the landing maneuver to driving down a freeway at ninety miles per hour with a blanket over the windshield. Sure, it could be done, but it was very tricky.

During Alan's first attempt at a night landing he followed step-by-step Doc Abbot's instructions for landing the Corsair. He approached the rear of the dimly lit outline of the *FDR* in a steep banking turn to the left, so that he could get his bearings through the side window of the plane's cockpit. Once he had lined up his Corsair with the deck of the ship, he straightened the plane, dropped its nose, throttled back, and descended toward the deck, his hands and feet firmly on the controls. Even a slight movement of the controls at that moment could send the Corsair careening into the ocean or, worse, nosefirst into the deck. All the while Alan's eyes scanned the plane's instrument panel and the fast-approaching deck of the *FDR*, looking for the LSO's lighted signal paddles. As soon as he saw the paddles drop, Alan pulled the plane's nose up while cutting the throttle. This maneuver "dropped" the plane onto the deck with a thud, where the tailhook would, hopefully, catch one of the arresting wires that ran across the flight deck and pull the Corsair to an abrupt halt. Alan described these landings as being more like a controlled crash than a landing.

Alan won the distinction of being the first nugget in the United States Navy to safely land his airplane on an aircraft-carrier deck at night. The experience whet Alan's appetite for more challenges.

After plying the aqua blue Caribbean waters for several months, the *FDR* returned to Norfolk from its shakedown cruise. The vessel was then assigned to depart in September for a tour of duty with

American forces in the Mediterranean Sea. But before the *FDR* set sail for the Mediterranean, Alan and his shipmates were granted some very welcome shore leave. Alan spent his leave getting reacquainted with his now-one-year-old daughter.

Then on September 13, 1948, duty—and adventure—called. The USS *Franklin D. Roosevelt* steamed out of Norfolk, Virginia, and headed across the vast Atlantic Ocean for Europe. Once at sea, Alan quickly readjusted to the routine of shipboard life as one of the four thousand members of the *FDR*'s crew. But unlike the sailors, Alan always focused his attention on the airplanes parked on the bow of the ship in neat rows. Every day he walked by the planes and checked that their wheels were properly blocked and that they were securely strapped down. In the event of an approaching storm, the airplanes would be moved to the rear of the main flight deck, where they would be safer.

Somehow, as they approached the Azores, nine hundred miles west of Portugal, the ship's meteorologist failed to notice a huge storm brewing. By the time the storm engulfed the *FDR*, it was too late to relocate the airplanes to the rear of the deck. The wind began to howl and soon turned the gray, icy-cold water of the Atlantic into a frothing cauldron. The ship began to pitch and roll, and the crew were ordered below deck. Alan hunkered down on his bunk and listened to the sound of the engines as they strained to keep the ship headed forward into the wind and waves. He would feel the ship rise as it crept up the side of an oncoming wave and then feel the vessel shudder and vibrate as it careened down the back side of the wave.

The ship's pattern of up and down, shudder and vibrate, seemed to go on for hours. Alan learned from an officer who had been on duty on the bridge that some of the waves the FDR was riding over were up to forty feet high, and as they crashed by the ship, they would send sheets of water flooding across the deck. Alan inquired as to how the squadron's planes were faring on deck. The officer assured him they were a little waterlogged but that they were tied down securely and had not moved an inch, in spite of the howling wind and mountainous sea.

Not too long afterward, Alan felt the FDR begin to rise as it encountered another wave. But this time the ship just seemed to keep going up and up. Then finally the bow pitched violently forward while the vessel's steel hull groaned with the strain. Then the ship began to rise again before settling back. From his experience aboard the USS Cogswell in the Pacific during World War II, Alan knew that the FDR had just encountered an enormous rogue wave.

Alan immediately began to worry about his Corsair, lashed down on the front of the flight deck. The plane was already in a precarious position in relation to the waves the FDR had been encountering. What would a huge wave like the one they had just endured do to the plane? Alan, along with the other squadron members, soon learned the answer to the question. The huge wave had submerged the front of the flight deck and washed overboard eleven of the squadron's aircraft, including Alan's Corsair. Alan could scarcely believe it. His plane was now at the bottom of the Atlantic Ocean. This was a depressing thought.

Finally the storm subsided, and Alan was able to go up on deck and see for himself the situation with the squadron's airplanes. Sure enough, eleven planes were missing, and several of those that had not been swept overboard were so badly damaged that they would never fly again. The *FDR* steamed on toward the Mediterranean, her crew in a somber mood. The ship was, after all, an aircraft carrier, but it had very few flight-ready, intact aircraft aboard.

Chapter 8

Test Pilot

The next three months were frustrating for Alan and the other naval pilots aboard the *FDR* as they waited patiently for replacement airplanes to arrive. With no planes to fly, the men had little to do, and they spent much of their time huddled below deck as they sailed across the Mediterranean. When the *FDR* eventually arrived in Greece, replacement airplanes were waiting for them there.

Soon Alan was back in the air in a new Corsair. But while he had been stranded on an aircraft carrier without a plane to fly, much to his chagrin, things had not been standing still in the world of military aviation. Back in the United States, navy and air force pilots were flying experimental jet planes and were routinely breaking the sound barrier and setting new flying records. In addition, the navy had established the Naval Test Pilot School at Patuxent River Naval Air Station in Maryland. The purpose of the school was to train an elite group of pilots to fly and test the limits of the new jet fighters that were coming into service in the military.

When Alan heard about the Naval Test Pilot School, he set his sights on attending it and learning to fly jets. His aspiration to do so was fueled when his squadron commander, Doc Abbot, was promoted to the Pentagon in Washington, D.C. Before Doc Abbot left for Washington, Alan began pressuring him to use whatever influence he had at the Pentagon to get him into the test pilot school. Turner Caldwell, a veteran World War II fighter pilot, then became commander of the flight squadron aboard the *FDR*. He and Alan developed a close relationship, and when Caldwell, too, was promoted to the Pentagon, Alan asked him to use his influence to get him into the school. Alan now had two allies well placed in the navy hierarchy, and he determined to pester them both on a regular basis until he was sitting in the cockpit of a fighter jet at the Naval Test Pilot School.

Meanwhile, Alan was reassigned to the aircraft carrier USS *Midway* to gain experience in cold-weather flying. He was glad for the change of pace and the opportunity to learn a new skill—flying while wearing a bulky, insulated suit, which was akin to a diver's wetsuit.

Alan returned to the United States from his duties aboard the USS *Midway* in May 1950. It was normal navy procedure for a pilot who had just completed a tour of duty aboard an aircraft carrier to be given a desk job for a while before his next flying assignment. However, when Alan opened his orders to see what his next assignment would be, he was delighted to see that he was being transferred to the U.S. Naval Test Pilot School at Patuxent River Naval Air Station. Doc Abbot and Turner Caldwell's influence at the Pentagon had paid off for him.

Alan and Louise and their daughter, Laura, moved to the Patuxent River Naval Air Station, or Pax as everyone called it, in the summer of 1950 and built a modest redbrick house on the shore of the Patuxent River. By now Louise was again pregnant and ready to settle down and be a family, though as she was quickly learning, being married to a naval aviator meant long periods alone at home while her husband was away on various tours of duty.

When he arrived at Pax, Alan discovered that at twenty-six years of age he was once again the youngest member of the twenty-four-person test-pilot class. Undeterred, he threw himself into his studies, which for the first five months consisted of a course of intensive classroom study in such things as aerodynamics, physics, and mathematics, as well as the fundamentals of flying jet airplanes.

Alan's arrival at Pax coincided with the start of another war on the other side of the world on the Korean Peninsula. At the end of World War II the Korean Peninsula was divided into two separate countries, North Korea and South Korea. The North was Communist and was supported by the Soviet

Union and China, while the United States and her allies supported the democratic South. But on June 25, 1950, North Korean troops invaded South Korea. In response, the United States and a group of allies, under the auspices of the United Nations, declared war on North Korea. For the next three years the Korean Peninsula would be at war as UN forces tried to contain the Communist North.

For the first time, the battle in the air over Korea was fought using jet fighters, with North Korean pilots flying Soviet-built MiG jets. As a result, the U.S. Navy was trying to introduce jets into its fighter squadrons as fast as possible. This is where the Test Pilot School came in. The navy needed to know the physical limits of its new aircraft while flying so that pilots could be instructed in how to fly them and what actions to take in case of an emergency.

After his five months of classroom study, Alan took to the skies. His job was to test prototypes of the latest jet fighters to see how far they could be pushed before they malfunctioned, spun out of control, or exploded in midair. Often there were no updated flight manuals on the planes, and the test pilots had to "feel" their way along in the air.

Each day and each flight could be Alan's last, or the last for any of his equally brave fellow test pilots. But with the Korean War in full swing, any new information gleaned from these dangerous flights about a particular jet's capabilities could mean the difference between life and death for a pilot patrolling the skies over the Korean Peninsula.

Alan's favorite assignment was testing the F2H-2 Banshee, a twin-engine, straight-winged jet. The plane was twice as powerful as its predecessor, the FH-1 Phantom, and Alan felt exhilarated when he opened the Banshee's throttle and hurtled along close to the speed of sound.

Sometimes tests did not go according to plan, and that was what happened on one particular test flight. The plan was to see whether a jet could fly carrying ten thousand pounds of bombs. To lighten the load of the jet as it got off the ground, the plane would take off with its fuel tank nearly empty and then refuel once airborne. Bob Elder, Alan's superior, would fly the Banshee jet with the bombs, and Alan would take off in his jet and fly alongside Bob, observing the test and acting as a safety plane.

A tanker airplane took off first, followed by Alan, and then Bob in the bomb-laden Banshee. Once airborne, the two jets quickly caught up to the slower propeller-driven tanker plane. Alan refueled his jet first.

Refueling in midair was a precise maneuver. Alan had to bring his jet up behind the tanker plane, flying just a few feet below it, and adjust his speed so that the two planes were flying at the same speed, mere feet apart. Alan then extended a pipe, called a probe, from his jet and maneuvered his plane until the probe was inserted into the drogue, a funnel-like opening on the end of a pipe that extended from the tanker plane. Once the probe and drogue were inserted into each other, fuel flowed from the tanker into the fuel tank of

Alan's jet. When he had taken on sufficient fuel, Alan backed off his jet, and the probe and drogue were disconnected. However, Alan was unaware that as he backed off, the tip of his probe had damaged the drogue.

It was now Bob Elder's turn to bring the Banshee in and refuel it. As Alan had done, Bob matched the tanker's speed and altitude and maneuvered his probe into the damaged drogue. But because of the damage, instead of fuel flowing into the tank of Bob's Banshee, it gushed out all over the jet. The fuel was quickly sucked into the intake duct for the engine, where it ignited. Bob's Banshee was soon a fireball that rolled over in the air and began falling toward the ground.

Alan watched the scene in horror. He tried to contact Bob on the radio, but it was dead. There was no doubt in Alan's mind that Bob's plane was going to crash. Alan followed the plane down, staying far enough away to avoid the burning balls of fuel spraying off the Banshee, and waited for the inevitable impact with the ground.

Much to Alan's surprise, however, somehow, about three hundred feet above the ground, Bob managed to regain control of his crippled Banshee and bring it in for a rough but safe landing at a nearby airfield. Alan wouldn't be getting a new superior officer after all.

Not long after the refueling incident, Alan was assigned a new challenge. This time he had to figure out the best way to land a Banshee if it was disabled and lost power in flight, either through its engine flaming out or by being hit from enemy fire. There was only one way to find out how to land the Banshee should this situation occur, and that was to fly high in a Banshee, cut off the engine, allow the plane to go into a spin, and then see whether it was possible to keep control of the aircraft and bring it in for a safe landing.

The test was carried out in 1952 at Muroc Airbase at Muroc Lake in California, the site where five years before air force pilot Chuck Yeager had become the first man to fly faster than the speed of sound. Alan flew his jet up to a height of forty thousand feet and cut the engine. He then guided the plane down to the ground in what was known as a dead-stick landing. It was a dangerous maneuver, since the Banshee was not designed to land without its engine running and the lack of jet thrust altered the plane's dynamics in the air. Still, Alan made a series of dead-stick landings, each time managing to bring the jet down safely. He discovered that the way to bring the plane in to land was to make a long, slow, controlled descent. When the test was complete, he compiled a detailed report, laying out the procedure a pilot should follow should his jet lose power during flight.

As nerve-racking as these assignments were, Alan loved being a test pilot. He did not, however, tell Louise all the details of his daily adventures, especially after their second daughter, whom they named Julie, was born. Louise preferred to stay in the background, looking after the children and taking an active role in church life.

During his time as a navy test pilot, Alan earned a reputation as an exemplary pilot who could fly almost any kind of airplane. However, Alan did have a tendency to show off. He loved to fly in low and at full speed over such things as a beach where people were sunbathing in New Jersey, over the parade ground at the Naval Aviation Ordnance Center on Chincoteague Island, Virginia, and anywhere else he could show off his skill as a pilot. Sometimes his unofficial antics got him in trouble. He was grounded twice, and two letters of reprimand were placed in his personnel file. And after Alan buzzed the parade ground at Chincoteague Island, Admiral Alfred Pride was so enraged that he threatened to have Alan court-martialed. And Alan would have been if his two superior officers, Bob Elder and John Hyland, had not interceded on his behalf and convinced the admiral that Alan was too good a pilot to be dismissed from the navy.

Early in 1953, Alan's life took another turn. The Korean War had dragged on long enough for many of the jet fighters that Alan had tested to be mass-produced and placed into service in the navy. Now a new aircraft-carrier jet squadron was being assembled to fight in Korea, and Alan was picked to be one of the pilots in the new squadron. He accepted the job, eager to fly in combat the planes he knew so well.

Knowing that he would probably not be returning to the Patuxent River Naval Air Station, Alan settled Louise and the girls in Palo Alto, California. With his family settled, he climbed aboard the USS

Oriskany to join his new squadron, VF-193, better known as the Ghost Riders.

Alan was introduced to his new commanding officer, James Ramage, whom everyone called Jig Dog. He soon learned that Jig Dog was a hands-on commander who loved to fly with his men rather than shuffle paperwork and bark out orders. Alan liked the man from their first meeting, and Jig Dog soon recognized what a talented aviator and leader Alan was.

Alan's first opportunity to shine came when he realized that most of his fellow pilots were not very good at landing their Banshees on the *Oriskany's* deck. Huge gouges in the teak planks of the flight deck testified to the fact.

The main problem, Alan soon realized, was that the pilots were bringing their new jets in too high and too fast on landing approach and then cutting engine power, causing their planes to come down hard on the flight deck, damaging the teak planking in the process. With his experience flying jets in all sorts of risky situations, Alan set to work teaching the men of the squadron how to bring the planes in lower and slower on their landing approach while avoiding stalling. Then, when they cut power, the jets would float down to the deck for a much gentler landing. Alan's instruction paid off. Soon the members of the squadron were making much better landings that led to the teak planking of the flight deck rarely having to be replaced.

As the twenty-seven-thousand-ton USS *Oriskany* plowed its way across the Pacific Ocean toward

Asia, Alan and other members of the squadron carefully read each dispatch about the course of the war in Korea. It appeared from these dispatches that the United Nations was getting close to signing an armistice with North Korea and China. While this was good news to almost everyone, Alan was disappointed. He hoped that the *Oriskany* would arrive off Korea before the fighting stopped. More than anything else, he wanted to test himself in combat against the Soviet-built MiGs flown by the North Koreans. But it was not to be. On July 27, 1953, just as the USS *Oriskany* arrived off the coast of South Korea, a cease-fire was signed and the fighting on the Korean Peninsula stopped. Alan was bitterly disappointed. There would be no dog-fights with enemy aircraft for him. Instead he flew routine patrols, mostly over the 38th parallel, the border between North and South Korea.

One night, as a storm approached, Alan was flying a solo mission out over the Sea of Japan when he received word from the *Oriskany* that unidentified aircraft had been spotted on the ship's radar. He was dispatched to go and find out whom the planes belonged to. As it turned out, the unidentified planes were U.S. Air Force jets. Alan turned his plane around and headed back to the *Oriskany*. But as he descended through the clouds, he descended into the heart of the storm. Wind buffeted his Banshee, and rain lashed against the cockpit windshield so that he could see nothing and was forced to fly by his instruments. Then disaster struck. A bolt of lightning hit Alan's plane, knocking out his navigation system and radio and damaging several other systems. He was left with only his skill as a pilot and navigator to find his way back to the USS *Oriskany.*

Alan nursed the Banshee to where he thought the *Oriskany* should be. But when he got there, he could see no sign of the ship. Despite the fact that his fuel was low, he stayed calm and composed and banked left, and then left again, in a series of ever-increasing squares—a search pattern—all the while squinting through the rain-drenched cockpit window for any sign of the carrier below.

Just when he began to fret that he would have to ditch his Banshee in the sea, Alan made out a dim red light below. As he brought his jet in low, he could make out the dark outline of the *Oriskany.* But landing on an aircraft carrier in a storm at night was no easy task as the vessel pitched and rolled on the tempestuous sea. Sometimes the flight deck could rise and fall thirty feet or more as the ship rode over a wave. Almost out of fuel, Alan had no option but to attempt a landing in the dark. He lined up his plane with the outline of the ship, lowered his landing gear, and powered back the throttle, all the while hoping and praying that the ship did not rise on a wave as he approached, causing him to crash in a fireball into the stern of the vessel instead of dropping onto the flight deck. However, the carrier did not rise as he approached. Alan was never more relieved to feel the thud of his wheels against the flight deck than he was that night.

More excitement soon followed, though this time it was Jig Dog's life, not Alan's, that was in danger. As part of their ongoing battle-readiness training, Alan's squadron was going to make a simulated attack on the battleship USS *Iowa,* which was steaming nearby. On March 15, 1954, in the pre-dawn icy morning, the squadron began taking off from the deck of the *Oriskany.* Alan was surprised that his commanders had decided to go ahead with the exercise. Not only was it icy cold, but also heavy snow began to fall as the planes were taking off. Still, once he was airborne in his Banshee, Alan fell into place off the left wing of Jig Dog's Banshee. As his commander, Doc Abbot, had done on the *FDR,* James Ramage had chosen Alan to be his wingman.

Once all of the planes were airborne from the *Oriskany,* Jig Dog took the lead as the squadron followed him toward the *Iowa.* Things seemed to be going normally with the mission when Alan noticed that Jig Dog was beginning to veer off course and then proceeded to go into a sharp banking turn. Alan, along with the rest of the squadron followed his leader. But when Jig Dog failed to pull out of the banking turn, Alan became worried. "CAG! CAG!" (Navy lingo for commander air group) he called over his radio.

Alan waited for a reply, but there was none. "CAG! CAG!" he yelled again over the radio. "Nose down! Nose down, CAG! Wings level. You're going in!"

Slowly Jig Dog leveled out his plane. But when he spoke over the radio, he sounded slurred and dis-oriented. Alan knew something was seriously wrong.

At the same time a call came over the radio canceling the exercise because of the weather. Alan then concentrated on getting his commander safely back to the ship. He continued talking over the radio to Jig Dog, and as they got closer to the ship, he began to notice his commander was becoming more coherent. They talked over the landing, and then Alan turned aside while Jig Dog lined up his Banshee on approach to the *Oriskany*. Moments later, Jig Dog's plane was safely on the carrier's deck, and Alan breathed a sigh of relief.

After he had landed, Alan discussed with Jig Dog what had gone wrong. Apparently the oxygen supply to the commander's face mask had failed, though Jig Dog was unaware of it at the time. And when the windshield of his Banshee had frozen over, he cranked up the heat in the cockpit to thaw it out. The excessive heat in the cockpit and lack of oxygen had conspired to disorient Jig Dog. The commander said that he would have surely crashed if it hadn't been for Alan's voice over the radio. Somehow Alan's words *You're going in!* had snapped Jig Dog out of his stupor enough for him to level off the Banshee and follow Alan's instructions.

Alan was just glad that Jig Dog had survived the ordeal. He and his commander had become close during their time together on the USS *Oriskany*. Twice in recent days Alan had stayed cool and collected under extreme conditions. This trait would serve him well in the unimaginable challenges that lay just ahead.

Chapter 9

Sputniks and Kaputniks

Six months after Alan had saved Jig Dog's life, his two tours of duty aboard the USS *Oriskany* came to an end, but not before he had been promoted. It was an achievement Alan was proud of: at only thirty years of age he was already Lieutenant Commander Shepard. It took most naval officers fifteen years to attain that rank, but Alan had done it in ten.

After leaving the *Oriskany*, Alan was transferred back to the Patuxent River Naval Air Station in Maryland to serve once again as a test pilot and as an instructor at the test-pilot school. Once again the Shepard family moved across the country.

During 1956, as a test pilot, Alan found himself climbing into the cockpit of a Grumman F11F Tiger. The F11F Tiger was a newly developed jet fighter being tested for deployment by the navy. However, the plane exhibited an unusual characteristic during flight. If a pilot tried to turn the Tiger when it was flying faster than the speed of sound—around 750 miles per hour—the plane tended to turn in the opposite direction and then spin out of control. Alan had been called upon to fly the plane and see whether he could work out how a pilot could stop this from happening and control the plane during high-speed turns or suggest design changes that might alleviate the problem.

Alan's test flight of the F11F Tiger was conducted at the former Muroc Air Base, which had been renamed Edwards Air Force Base, located an hour north and east of Los Angeles, on the edge of the Mojave Desert. As he strapped himself into the Tiger, Alan thought about how far aviation had come during his lifetime. When he was in high school, it had seemed impossible that a manned aircraft could ever break the sound barrier. Scientists speculated that even if such a plane could be built, the pilot flying it would not survive but would be crushed to death by the forces on him, like a bug on a windshield. But that had not been the case. Such an airplane could be and was built, and in 1947 the sound barrier had been broken without the pilot's ending up like a squashed bug. Instead planes had continued to go faster and faster, and now, in 1956, the Tiger, the airplane Alan was about to test, could fly at Mach 2, twice the speed of sound. And Alan knew that planes would continue to go faster as bigger and better jet engines were developed and as airplane design improved.

After he had strapped himself in and adjusted his seat harness, Alan checked his instruments in a preflight check. He planned a smooth, spiraling ascent in the Tiger to an altitude of sixty thousand feet, which he calculated should take him close to an hour to climb to. Once he reached that altitude, he would put the F11F Tiger into a dive and see whether it would spin out of control, as it had for other pilots.

Everything on the ascent went according to plan, and when he reached sixty thousand feet, Alan dropped the Tiger's nose, put it into a dive toward the ground over eleven miles below, and opened the throttle to full. The aircraft began to gather speed rapidly and was soon approaching the speed of sound. When the Tiger reached Mach 1, the engine suddenly and unexpectedly flamed out and the plane lost power. Without power, the glass canopy that covered the cockpit quickly began to freeze over, obscuring Alan's line of vision, and the Tiger began to drop toward the ground like a stone or, as Alan later explained it, "like a Steinway piano."

Alan managed to wrestle with the control stick and stop the aircraft from spinning completely out of control, but he was still falling fast. Calling on his mental and physical reserves, Alan forced himself to stay focused. He let the Tiger free-fall ten thousand feet and then made an attempt to restart the engines. He reasoned that by letting the jet fall lower, the air would be getting thicker and he would have more chance of starting the engines. But when he tried to restart the engines, nothing happened.

Alan stayed calm and primed the fuel pump for another attempt to restart the engines. Still they did not start. Now Alan was beginning to get concerned. The ground was approaching fast. It was time for Alan to bail out of the Tiger and parachute to the ground while the plane crashed in the desert.

Alan decided to make one last attempt to restart the engines before he bailed out, if he could by then. Again he primed the fuel pump and quickly went through the start-up procedure for the engines. This time the engines whirred to life. At twelve thousand feet, Alan was able to gain back control of the Tiger and pull it out of its perilous dive, but not before he had free-fallen forty-eight thousand feet, just over nine miles. Alan was very relieved when he finally felt the wheels of the Tiger thump down onto the runway at Edwards Air Force Base.

Needless to say, Alan wrote a scathing report about the lack of airworthiness of the F11F Tiger and recommended that the navy cancel all future orders for the plane. The navy followed his recommendation, and no more than the 199 Tigers, which the navy had already taken delivery of, were purchased. Of course the Grumman Aircraft Company was not at all happy about Alan's recommendation, but Alan did not care. To him the safety of navy pilots was the most important thing.

Soon after wrestling with the F11F Tiger in the clear sky over Southern California, Alan and Louise faced a challenge of a different sort. Louise's mother called to say that Louise's sister Adele had died after a sudden illness, leaving two sons and a daughter behind. Adele's husband was unable to look after the children, and the burden for their care rested on Mr. and Mrs. Brewer.

Louise drove herself and her two girls to Longwood Gardens, the DuPont family estate in Philadelphia, where her father was still the head of maintenance, to see how she could help. She soon discovered that the three children were too much for her aging parents to deal with. The two boys, who were older, were sent off to boarding school, but Alice, who was six years old, was too young to be sent away to school.

After many discussions, Alan and Louise decided to bring Alice back to live with them at Patuxent River Naval Air Station and raise her as their own daughter. This required a lot of adjustment on everyone's part, especially for their daughter Julie, who was the same age as Alice.

In July 1957, there were more changes ahead for the Shepard family. Alan was asked to enroll at the Naval War College in Newport, Rhode Island. At first he resisted the notion; the last thing he wanted to do was to sit in a classroom when he could be flying. But the more he thought about it, the more he came to see what a great opportunity attending the Naval War College was. The navy's most elite officers had all attended the college. Alan realized that this was an important step in advancing to a higher rank in the navy, perhaps even commanding his own fighter squadron, or even becoming an admiral. Once again the Shepard family packed up and moved, this time from Maryland to Newport, Rhode Island.

Alan was only one month into his studies at the Naval War College when, on October 4, 1957, a 183-pound, basketball-sized metal ball captured his and the world's attention. The metal ball was called Sputnik. It was the world's first artificial earth-orbiting satellite, and it had been launched by Soviet Russia, not the United States.

Sputnik took about ninety-eight minutes to orbit the earth, and as it did so, it transmitted a series of beeps on a shortwave radio band. The fact that a Soviet satellite was circling overhead caught America by surprise. And it certainly caught Alan Shepard by surprise. He had read in the newspaper that the Russians couldn't seem to be able to build washing machines, refrigerators, and other appliances that worked properly, but somehow they had managed to build a satellite and a rocket to launch it and had also managed to get it into space. Alan was stunned.

While Alan had been riding the crest of the wave of developments in aviation, another group of scientist and engineers, in both the Soviet Union and the United States, had been quietly working away on another technology—rockets.

During World War II, scientists in Nazi Germany had built the V-2, a liquid-propelled rocket that had a bomb attached to its nose. The Nazis had used the V-2 to bomb the city of London. At the end of the war, the Soviets and the Americans had gathered up the scientists who had created the V-2 and shipped them to Russia and the United States to begin working on developing rockets for both countries. Among the German rocket scientists who came to the United States was Wernher von Braun, the director of the V-2 program for the Nazis.

When, soon after the war, the Russians developed their own atomic bombs, and then nuclear bombs, a race began among the rocket scientists in both Russia and the United States to build a rocket that could carry a nuclear bomb. It was a race that the Russians won in early 1957, developing a rocket that could fly from Russia all the way across Europe and the Atlantic Ocean to the United States.

Having won that race, the Soviets had turned their attention to launching an artificial satellite into orbit, and they were successful at this too.

After hearing of the launch of Sputnik, Alan learned that the satellite was visible to the naked eye as it orbited the earth. Late one night, after the girls and Louise had gone to bed, he went out into the backyard of the small cottage the family lived in on the grounds of the Naval War College and scanned the night sky. Finally he spotted the faint glow of Sputnik in the sky above him as it made its way over the United States on one of its orbits of the earth. "That little rascal," he muttered to himself as he watched. Alan was filled with a surge of emotions. He was amazed to be seeing a man-made satellite orbiting the earth, but he was also angry that it was the Soviet Union and not the United

States that had planned it, built it, and launched it into space.

Alan's anger and frustration only grew when, a month later, on November 3, 1957, the Soviet Union launched a second satellite, Sputnik 2, into orbit. Gleeful, the Soviet leader, Nikita Khrushchev, announced that not only was Sputnik 2 bigger than Sputnik 1, weighing in at 250 pounds, but also it contained a cabin, and in that cabin it carried a live dog named Laika. Americans began to worry. If the Soviets could keep a dog alive in space, would humans be next? Had the United States lost the battle for supremacy in space before the race had even started? And if the Russians could put satellites into space that could orbit over the United States, would it be long before they adapted those satellites to carry nuclear bombs aimed at America? People began to clamor for the government to do something about the situation.

What the U.S. government did was try to launch its own satellite into space. However, all did not go well. On December 6, 1957, at Cape Canaveral in Florida, a Vanguard rocket blasted off with a three-and-a-half-pound satellite in its nose. The Vanguard rocket rose four feet into the air and then sank back to the launchpad and exploded in a massive fireball. To make matters worse, the launch was televised for the world to see!

It was not until January 31, 1958, that the United States finally succeeded in launching its first satellite into orbit. The satellite was called Explorer I, and it was launched atop a modified

Redstone rocket developed by Wernher von Braun and his team of scientists and engineers. The race for supremacy in space had begun.

With the successful launch of Explorer I, the United States attempted to launch more satellites into orbit. But like the spectacular debacle of Vanguard, most of these attempts ended in failure. These satellites had impressive names like Thor, Matador, and Hound Dog, but with each successive failure, newspaper reporters began referring to them as "Kaputnik," "Flopnik," and "Stayputnik."

Meanwhile, Alan kept busy with his studies at the Naval War College, though he kept up with the news of the space race. In early October 1958, he read about the formation of what was being called the National Aeronautics and Space Administration, or NASA for short. The preamble to the Act of Congress that established NASA stated that its purpose was "to provide for research into the problems of flight within and outside the Earth's atmosphere, and for other purposes."

The new National Aeronautics and Space Administration agency absorbed the earlier National Advisory Committee for Aeronautics and its eight thousand employees and one-hundred-million-dollar annual budget, along with three major research laboratories—the Langley Aeronautical Laboratory, Ames Aeronautical Laboratory, and Lewis Flight Propulsion Laboratory—and two smaller test facilities. Soon after its founding, NASA was expanded to incorporate other organizations, including the space-science group of the Naval

Research Laboratory in Maryland, the army's Jet Propulsion Laboratory managed by the California Institute of Technology, and the Army Ballistic Missile Agency in Huntsville, Alabama, where Wernher von Braun and his team were engaged in developing large rockets.

At the same time NASA was being formed, Alan graduated from the Naval War College in Newport, Rhode Island, and was transferred to the navy's Atlantic Fleet Headquarters in Norfolk, Virginia, where he was given the job of aircraft readiness officer. If everything went according to plan, Alan hoped to work his way up in the command structure of the Atlantic Fleet. However, Alan's carefully made plans were about to be blasted sky-high.

Chapter 10

Astronauts

Alan reread the announcement he had ripped from the *New York Times* which outlined the minimum standards for a whole new classification of men. NASA was calling these men "astronauts," from the Greek words for space and sailor. These astronauts would be the first men to leave the earth's gravitational pull and fly into outer space. The article declared, "Each man must have at least fifteen hundred hours of logged flight time; jet pilot training, experience, and full qualifications; at least a bachelor's degree for academic qualifying; and he must pass national security requirements. He may not be taller than five feet eleven inches, he must weight less than one hundred eighty pounds, and must be under forty years of age."

By now Alan knew the qualifications by heart, and word around the navy base at Norfolk was that NASA had begun sending out invitations to 110 of the top test pilots from the U.S. Navy, Marine Corps, and Air Force to try out to become one of the six members of the new astronaut corps. *Surely, I'll get an invitation to try out,* Alan mumbled to himself.

A week passed, however, and no invitation from NASA had arrived on Alan's desk. Other pilots in the building had received their invitations two days before, and Alan was sure that all the invitations would have been sent out together. So why hadn't he gotten one?

By Friday afternoon he was agitated about the whole situation as he packed up and headed to the parking lot. He hoped he wouldn't have to talk to anyone there, as he had little to say, or at least little that was wise to say about NASA at that point. He still could not understand how, if NASA wanted the best test pilots in the United States, it had not invited him to try out. He fumed as he slammed the car door shut and shot out of the parking lot on his way home.

Alan stayed mad all weekend. He did not want to read the newspaper in case there was more information from NASA about the astronaut program, and he didn't want to go to play golf in case he ran into someone who was part of the elite 110 test pilots.

On Monday morning Alan returned to work, hoping to keep busy on his latest project and to forget about the rejection he felt at not receiving an invitation from NASA. Just as he sat down at his desk, a junior staffer tapped on his door. "Sir, I have an envelope for you," the young man said, looking ill at ease. "It's stamped with last week's date. It must have been misplaced."

Alan took one look at the words "Top Secret" stamped on the envelope with the large NASA logo and didn't know whether to whoop for joy or reprimand the junior staffer who had misplaced the valuable invitation.

The invitation contained instructions on the selection process. It stated that the 110 pilots invited to participate had been divided into three random groups and that groups one and two were to report to the Pentagon in Washington, D.C., for a briefing. The third group was being held in reserve in case six suitable men could not be found in the first two groups.

Alan heaved a sign of relief when he discovered that his name was listed in the first group. A week later he was sitting with sixty-eight other pilots at the Pentagon. They had all been ordered to wear civilian clothes to the briefing in order to keep the meeting secret. Alan listened intently as Dr. Robert Gilruth, Director of the Space Task Group, spoke to them about the selection process. Dr. Gilruth pointed out that the selection process would be grueling and would include severe physical and psychological tests in order to find out who were the most physically and mentally tough men in the room. Alan looked around, sure that he would make the cut but also realizing that every one of his competitors in the room probably felt the same way.

Before leaving at the end of the meeting, each man underwent a brief interview and was asked whether given what he now knew about the astronaut program, he still wanted to volunteer for the program, and why. Alan was at the biggest crossroads of his life. If he volunteered and was accepted into the program, he knew that he would be taking himself off the promotion track he was on to become an admiral in the navy. But for what? No man had ever been into space, and Laika, the lone Soviet space dog aboard Sputnik 2, had never returned. Sputnik 2 had been a one-way mission. Would NASA do the same thing? How much chance did an astronaut have of a successful launch, mission into space, and reentry into the earth's atmosphere? And what would happen to a man in space, anyway? Some newspaper reports speculated that men would suffer blindness, heart attacks, digestive failure, even brain damage, from the effects of zero gravity on the body. Yet despite all of the potential risks, only ten men chose to drop out that day, and Alan Shepard was not one of them.

A few days later Alan was recalled by NASA for a more extensive interview, after which he was invited, along with thirty-two other men, to a testing facility in Albuquerque, New Mexico.

The testing in Albuquerque, carried out under the watchful eye of Dr. Randolph Lovelace, lived up to its promise of being grueling and sometimes inhumane. For over twelve hours a day for a week

Alan had every part of his body poked and prodded. Doctors took blood samples, urine samples, and stool samples. They scraped the back of his throat and shined a light into his eyes, ears, nose, and any other opening they could see into. They tested how his muscles responded when an electric current was passed through them, measured the contents of his stomach, gave him enemas, and submerged him in a tank of water to measure his total body volume. They were constantly taking his blood pressure and pulse and checking his brain-wave activity.

Although the testing was grueling and often humiliating, Alan persevered. He understood NASA's desire to find the best possible men to become astronauts. At the end of the week in Albuquerque, the men were sent on to Wright-Patterson Air Force Base in Dayton, Ohio, for more tests.

Alan was again poked and prodded. He had cold water squirted into his ears, sat for an hour with his feet in a bucket of ice water, and sat for two hours in a room heated to 135 degrees Fahrenheit. He was made to sit in a darkened, soundproof isolation chamber for hours on end, and he endured a machine that shook and pounded his body to mimic the effects of the extreme forces of flying.

None of this, however, was as challenging to Alan as the battery of psychological tests he had to undergo. Since he had never found it easy to analyze his feelings and emotions and understand what was going on in his mind, the 566-question personality inventory test was excruciating as he tried to analyze himself and describe his feelings.

And then he was asked to submit twenty different answers to the question "Who am I?"

Finally, much to Alan's relief, the testing came to an end. Surprisingly, only one of the candidates had flunked out of the tests, leaving thirty-one men who were considered mentally and physically fit enough to withstand the rigors of spaceflight, whatever that might entail.

A long period of waiting followed the tests while NASA officials made their final selection of six astronauts. It was not until Wednesday, April 1, 1959, that Alan received a phone call from an official at NASA. "We'd like you to join us," the official said. "Are you still willing to volunteer?"

"Ready and able!" Alan replied, aware that a huge grin was spreading across his face.

The official explained that choosing the first five men to be astronauts had been straightforward, but they had had difficulty making up their minds on the sixth man, so in the end they decided that there would be seven astronauts instead of six. He also informed Alan that NASA had decided to call the mission to send a man into space Project Mercury. Alan was instructed to be at a press conference to be held the following week at which the "Mercury Seven" would be introduced to the world. "Don't tell anyone except your immediate family about your selection until after the press conference," the official concluded. "You have to be prepared for some publicity."

When Alan got off the phone, he let out a huge whoop of joy, grabbed his jacket, and headed home

to tell Louise the good news. Louise seemed gen-
uinely happy for him, and the two of them agreed
what great timing the phone call had been. They
were flying to Boston that weekend for a family
wedding and would have the opportunity to tell
Alan's parents in person about his selection.

Things did not go quite the way Alan had hoped,
however, when he broke the news to his family. His
father, Bart, was upset that Alan had taken himself
off the fast track to becoming an admiral in the
navy and was willing to risk his life for something
as far-fetched as space travel. To him it sounded
more like something from a science-fiction comic
book than a well-chosen career path. Alan was hurt
by his father's reaction, but he knew what he
wanted—to be an American astronaut.

On April 9, 1959, a week and a day after receiving the phone call from NASA, Alan was seated
backstage in the ballroom of the Dolley Madison
House on Lafayette Square in Washington, D.C.,
NASA's temporary headquarters. Around him sat
six other men. Alan had met Marine Colonel John
Glenn, Navy Lieutenant Commander Wally Schirra,
and Navy Lieutenant Scott Carpenter during his
work as a test pilot, and he had met the other three
men, Air Force Captains Gordon Cooper, Gus
Grissom, and Deke Slayton, for the first time in
Albuquerque during their testing.

The men sat quietly, and Alan thought that, like
him, they were all sizing each other up. Yes, each of
the seven astronauts was a member of an elite
group of men, but each man knew that the other

astronauts were his competition in becoming the first man to go into space. As the men waited for the press conference to begin, Alan could feel the tension mounting, both in the seven astronauts backstage and among the throng of voices coming from the other side of the curtain.

Finally it was time to be introduced to the reporters, and a NASA official motioned for the seven men to follow him. As they made their way through the curtain, Alan turned to Deke Slayton, who was standing beside him dressed in a suit and bow tie, and said, "Those bow ties coming back into style?"

"What's wrong with my tie?" Deke retorted.

"Nothing, really," Alan said. "I doubt if the cameras will pick up that smeared egg or catsup or whatever that gunk is on it." A grin spread across his face as he watched Deke contort his head to try to see what was on his bow tie.

On the other side of the curtain the seven men were shown to the front of the ballroom. They sat down at a long table on which a microphone was positioned in front of each chair. On the floor in front of the table was a replica of an Atlas rocket and the Mercury capsule it would lift into space. When the men were seated, the NASA official announced, "Gentlemen, these are the astronaut volunteers. Take your pictures."

Suddenly the room erupted in activity as photographers rushed forward and pointed their cameras into the faces of the seven men. Flashbulbs began bursting all around, so many, in fact, that

Alan was soon seeing stars from the bright flashes. He didn't quite know what to make of all the activity, and he felt uncomfortable at being the center of so much attention. He looked around at Deke and Wally seated on either side of him and could see from the looks on their faces that they were feeling as he was. "I can't believe this. These people are nuts," he said so that both men could hear him. Deke and Wally nodded in agreement.

Finally, after what seemed like an eternity to Alan, the NASA official said, "Okay, ladies and gentlemen, please move back. Take your seats. Take your seats. Thank you."

Slowly the mob of reporters and photographers milling in front of the table retreated to their seats. As they did so, Alan noticed that Deke was still fiddling with his bow tie, so he elbowed him and said, "There's nothing on your tie, Slayton."

"What?" Deke questioned.

"Gotcha!" Alan said with a huge grin.

"What do you mean?" Deke asked, before the realization spread across his face that Alan had been kidding him about the gunk on his tie.

"Shepard, you—" Deke started to say, but his voice was drowned out by T. Keith Glennan, NASA's administrator, as he spoke into a microphone.

The administrator said, "It is my pleasure to introduce to you—and I consider it a very real honor, gentlemen—Malcolm S. Carpenter, Leroy G. Cooper, John H. Glenn Jr., Virgil I. Grissom, Walter M. Schirra Jr., Alan B. Shepard Jr., and Donald K. Slayton—the nation's Mercury astronauts."

The ballroom erupted in applause as reporters and photographers rose to their feet. Alan thought this was a funny reaction. Reporters were supposed to be objective. They weren't supposed to stand up and applaud the people they were about to question and report on.

Finally the applause died down, and the reporters and photographers took their seats. Now it was time for questions, and the first question floored Alan. A reporter asked, "What do your good ladies think of you becoming astronauts?"

Alan had expected questions about the challenges that lay ahead in putting a man into space, not a question about what Louise thought of his volunteering to become an astronaut. The question threw him off balance. "What I do is pretty much my business, professionwise. I have no problems at home," he stammered in reply when it came his turn to answer the question.

Similar questions followed, and each time Alan struggled to give an answer. He wondered whether anyone was going to ask questions about the challenges ahead. Those were the questions he could answer forthrightly.

While Alan searched haltingly for the right words to answer the questions the reporters asked, he noticed that John Glenn, unlike the other six astronauts, seemed to have no difficulty coming up with eloquent answers. But then, Alan told himself, what would you expect from a man who wrote poetry in the dark of the isolation chamber during testing at Wright-Patterson Air Force Base.

Finally the questions did turn to what lay ahead for the seven astronauts and the risks they faced, and these Alan found easier to answer, though not as well as John Glenn answered them.

After two hours of relentless questions from reporters, the news conference finally came to an end, much to Alan's relief. Alan and the other six members of the Mercury Seven left the Dolley Madison House totally clueless as to the movie-star-like status their introduction to the nation had instantly bestowed upon them.

Chapter 11

Under a Soviet Moon

At first Alan and Louise tried to laugh off the inconveniences of becoming the focus of so much media attention. Reporters and camera crews camped outside the Shepards' home in Virginia Beach and badgered Louise with questions such as "Does your husband have a suicide wish?" and "What will you do if Alan is blown up in a rocket accident?" Meanwhile Alan was followed by reporters everywhere he went, and photographers constantly popped off flashbulbs in his face as they snapped photos of one of the all-American pinup boys who was going to beat the Soviets into space. Despite the pressure of all this media attention, Alan, Louise, and their three girls tried to go about their normal routines, all the while hoping that the pesky reporters would eventually go away.

By the end of April everything was in place, and the Mercury program began in earnest. Alan and his six fellow astronauts were escorted to a large room at NASA's Langley Research Center, located at Hampton, Virginia, not far from Alan's home. Inside the room were eight metal, government-issue desks, one for each man and one for Nancy Lowe, the seventeen-year-old secretary who had been hired to do the office work for them all. Located in various buildings nearby were about thirty aerospace engineers who were about to tackle the daunting task of sending a man into space—and bringing him back safely.

The first task at hand for Alan and the other astronauts was to be briefed on progress so far with Project Mercury. Using a blackboard, the engineers sketched out diagrams and math equations as they laid out just how they intended to get a capsule into space, have it orbit the earth, and then have it reenter the atmosphere and land safely at sea, all without hurting or killing the astronaut inside the capsule. They talked of escape velocities and reentry trajectories, and Alan made notes as they spoke.

Other engineers explained about the equipment they would be using to get to space. The plan was to use an Atlas rocket being developed by the air force. On top of this rocket would be bolted the cone-shaped Mercury capsule, in which an astronaut would ride. Once the rocket had lifted the capsule into space, the capsule would separate from it and orbit the earth before reentering the earth's atmosphere. The capsule would reenter the atmosphere backwards, and its convex underside would be covered with a heat shield to withstand the heat generated by friction with the air. On top of the capsule was a parachute that would deploy as the capsule fell toward earth and guide it to a soft landing in the sea, where the navy would retrieve the astronaut and the capsule. And in case there was trouble with the launch of the rocket, an escape tower would be fitted to the top of the capsule. Several small rockets attached at the top of this tower would fire in case of emergency and pull the capsule free of the rocket.

Alan had to admit that it all sounded a little dangerous, but also exciting. Since no man had ever been into space before, no one was sure whether everything would work entirely as planned. Still, Alan was willing to take the risk.

During this time Alan also began to size up the other six astronauts. And he knew they were sizing him up too. Alan came to the conclusion that John Glenn was his greatest competitor among the group. Like him, John was an accomplished test pilot, and both men had accumulated fifty-five hundred hours of flying time, the most flying hours of any of the seven astronauts. And like Alan, John had loved the challenge of flying Corsairs before switching to jet fighters. The thing that John had, which Alan did not, was combat flying experience. Glenn had flown combat missions in both World War II and the Korean War, where he had shot down three Soviet-built MiG jet fighters. Alan made

a mental note to keep an eye on John Glenn in the
race to be the first man in space.

Three weeks into their training, on May 18,
1959, the Mercury Seven, along with a group of
NASA officials, traveled to Cape Canaveral, Florida,
to witness the launch of an Atlas rocket. A bright
sun shined overhead as Alan and the others took
their place on a viewing stand a half mile from the
launch site. Alan was impressed as the polished
steel skin of the rocket gleamed in the sun. The
Atlas D rocket was powered by a combination of liquid oxygen and RP-1 kerosene. The fuel was held
under pressure in tanks inside the rocket, with the
liquid oxygen cooled to minus 293 degrees
Fahrenheit, which caused ice to form on the outside skin of the rocket.

Eventually everything was ready, and the final
countdown began. When the countdown reached
zero, the engines of the Atlas D rocket burst to life
in a plume of fiery orange and billowing white
smoke. Seconds later Alan began to feel the power
of the rocket engines as a roar filled the air and the
platform they were standing on began to vibrate.
Slowly the Atlas began to lift into the clear Florida
sky as the Atlantic Ocean sparkled behind it. As it
rose, chunks of ice peeled off the side of the rocket
and fell back toward the ground. The sight of the
Atlas climbing into the sky awed Alan. But after the
rocket had reached an altitude of several hundred
yards, Alan noticed the nose of the Atlas D begin to
wobble. He had never seen a rocket launch this
close before and was not sure whether the wobble

was normal or not. Then the rocket began to tip sideways. Alan watched mesmerized as the skin of the rocket buckled and then the rocket exploded above their heads. The sky turned orange. Instinctively everyone on the viewing platform dived for cover. It took a moment for Alan to realize that the Atlas rocket was headed out over the Atlantic Ocean and the debris would fall there and not on him. He stood to his feet in stunned silence, as did the other astronauts, and watched as the last burning pieces of wreckage dropped into the sea. Finally Alan broke the silence. "Well, I'm glad they got that one out of the way. I sure hope they fix that!"

The next day the Mercury Seven attended a briefing on the Atlas launch failure at Cape Canaveral. But there was little that Alan and the other astronauts learned at the meeting. All the engineers and scientists could tell them was that they were studying photographs and telemetry data of the launch in hopes of learning what had caused the failure.

Despite the setback of the exploding Atlas D rocket, NASA and the Mercury Seven took things in stride and pressed on with the quest to put a man in space and return him safely to Earth. Meanwhile the rest of the country marveled at their resolve. But not Alan Shepard. For him risk was part of the job. He was a test pilot who had lived with the possibility of death every time he stepped into the cockpit. He accepted that accidents, and pilot deaths, were part of the learning process.

May 28, 1959, ten days after the failure of the
Atlas D rocket on launch, a Jupiter rocket safely
lifted off from Cape Canaveral and headed three
hundred miles into space. Then its nose cone
detached, reentered the earth's atmosphere, and
drifted down at the end of a parachute to a safe
landing in the Atlantic Ocean. Tucked inside the
capsule were two monkeys, Able and Baker. Both
animals had electrodes attached all over their bod-
ies so that scientists on the ground could monitor
how they reacted to the effects of weightlessness.
When the nose cone was recovered from the Atlantic,
both Able and Baker were still alive.

The readout from the electrodes on the two
monkeys showed that the animals did not suffer
from heart stoppages or from any of the other dire
things scientists had predicted could happen to a
man or animal in the weightlessness of space. Not
only that, the flight proved once and for all that it
was possible to launch a living being into space and
bring him back to Earth alive.

Alan and his fellow astronauts were glad to hear
this news, though they took a lot of ribbing from
people about following monkeys into space. Nonetheless, it was time for the Mercury Seven to begin
their flight training in earnest. While Alan had
thought that much of the flight training would
actually involve flying airplanes, he soon learned
that NASA had other ideas.

Soon Alan and the other six astronauts were
crisscrossing the country to various facilities where
they trained on an odd assortment of contraptions.

They traveled first to Wright-Patterson Air Force Base in Dayton, Ohio, to ride in the centrifuge machine there. This device consisted of a twenty-five-foot-long metal arm with a capsule about the size of the Mercury capsule attached to the end. Each astronaut took his turn in the capsule, which then spun, accelerating and decelerating as it did so, simulating the increased force of gravity (g-force) they would experience through blastoff and ascent into space and descent back to Earth. The purpose of the training was to get the astronauts familiar with the moves they would have to make during blastoff if there was trouble and the capsule had to make an emergency separation from the rocket.

Alan took his turn in the contoured seat inside the capsule and waited for the centrifuge to begin spinning. Suddenly the machine began to move, and in seconds everything outside the capsule was just a blur. Inside Alan could feel the increased gravity on his body, forcing him into the seat and making it hard for him to move his limbs. He concentrated hard, forcing his arms to make the various moves to operate the controls beside him. Over successive training sessions in the centrifuge, Alan slowly got the hang of what he would have to do in an emergency. And after each training session, he crawled out of the centrifuge so dizzy he would have to lie down for several minutes.

From Wright-Patterson, Alan traveled on to the Naval Air Development Center in Johnsville, Pennsylvania, where another centrifuge was located. A computer named Computer Typhoon, which filled a room half the size of a basketball court, controlled this centrifuge. The purpose of the time in this centrifuge was not to learn emergency procedures but to test the limits of g-forces on the astronauts. This centrifuge looked very much like the one at Wright-Patterson Air Force Base, only smaller. But as Alan soon learned, smaller didn't mean the machine was any easier on his body. Eventually at Johnsville, Alan got up to 16 g's (sixteen times the force of gravity on his body). At this force it was impossible to move. The extreme g-forces could easily push the blood out of a person's head, causing the person to black out and lose consciousness. To avoid this, Alan had to tense every muscle in his body so that the increased pressure in his body made it more difficult for the blood to flow from his head.

As if training time in two centrifuges was not enough, the astronauts traveled on to NASA's Lewis Research Center in Cleveland, Ohio. There a team of NASA engineers had constructed MASTIF, or Multi-Axis Space Training Inertial Facility. The contraption was unlike anything Alan had ever seen before. The gyroscope-like MASTIF consisted of three cages set inside one another and able to move independently of one another. One of the cages moved to simulate the effect of roll in the Mercury capsule, or its sideways tilt; another simulated pitch, the up-and-down movement of the nose; and the third cage simulated yaw, the motion around its vertical axis. At the center of the MASTIF was a cockpit, where an astronaut would sit strapped in tightly to his seat. The MASTIF could be operated with one, two, or all three of the cages in motion at once. It was the astronaut's job, using a control stick, to learn to control the device.

When it came his time to take a turn at the control of the MASTIF, Alan determined that he was going to be the first of the Mercury Seven to master the device. After he was safely strapped in to the cockpit, engineers began to rotate one, and then two, of the cages. The cockpit pitched and rolled, but slowly Alan got the hang of the control stick and, with quick flicks of his wrist, was eventually able to get the cockpit under control. Now feeling confident that he could control the contraption with all three cages spinning on their axes, Alan gave the engineers a thumbs-up. The engineers set all three cages in motion and soon had them spinning at full speed, thirty revolutions per second. The spinning cages made a deafening swishing sound as Alan desperately tried to bring the capsule under control. But try as he may, he could not seem to do it. Instead the cockpit spun out of control, with him inside. Finally, after only two minutes, Alan was forced to hit the "chicken switch" button that sounded a large horn and signaled the engineers to stop the machine. A dejected Alan Shepard was helped out of the cockpit and led to a nearby bed to lie down until his dizziness and nausea went away.

Later that afternoon Alan climbed back into the MASTIF for another try, and again he was forced to hit the chicken switch, as he had to do again the

next day. But with each session in the MASTIF he
was able to control the spinning cages a little better
until, after several days, he was able to master the
machine and get the cockpit under control at the
center of the three cages. Although it had taken
longer than he thought it would, Alan was the first
of the seven astronauts to master the MASTIF.

While the seven astronauts continued with their
training, NASA officials made an important decision. Given the problems they were having with the
Atlas rocket, the more reliable Redstone rocket
would be used to carry the first Mercury capsule
aloft. However, the Redstone was not as powerful as
the Atlas and so would not be able to lift the capsule high enough for it to go into orbit. As a result,
the first flight of the Mercury capsule would be suborbital, with the craft following a huge arch into
space and then back to Earth.

Since they were now going to use a Redstone
rocket, the Mercury Seven made their way to
Huntsville, Alabama, where rocket scientist Wernher
von Braun and his team had built the rocket. Von
Braun, a man in his late forties, with broad shoulders and sporting a mop of thick black hair,
showed them through the assembly plant and
introduced them to the intricacies of the Redstone
rocket, which he explained was an evolved version
of the V-2 rocket he had built for the Nazis. Later
the seven astronauts went to von Braun's home for
dinner with von Braun and his wife.

From the day the seven astronauts were introduced to the public and on through their training,

the news-media barrage did not let up. Alan and Louise began to use words like *invasion* and *unacceptable* to describe the press's intrusion into their lives. And Alan knew that the other six Mercury astronauts' families felt the same. None of them enjoyed the relentless attention or answering the same questions time after time for different news organizations. Something had to be done about the situation, and Alan for one was relieved when in July 1959, Walt Bonney, NASA's public-affairs officer, made a suggestion. Walt said he understood the interest of the news media in the space program. It was a legitimate story, but Walt also realized that the astronauts and their families were overwhelmed by all the media attention. Why didn't the Mercury Seven work exclusively with one news organization instead of with all of them? he asked. He suggested that the group have prominent lawyer Leo DeOrsey negotiate such a deal with a single news organization.

The astronauts and their wives met with DeOrsey at his country club outside Washington, D.C., where DeOrsey offered free legal services to them. The astronauts were delighted, especially when DeOrsey negotiated a deal with *Life* Magazine to exclusively tell the astronauts' story. What was even better, *Life* agreed to pay $500,000 for three years for the exclusive rights to the story, the money to be divided equally among the Mercury Seven. Alan quickly did the math in his head: he would be paid close to $24,000 a year for three years. That was much more than his current salary.

NASA officials and President Eisenhower approved the terms of the agreement. The September 14, 1959, issue of *Life* Magazine carried eighteen pages of stories and photographs of the astronauts and their families under the headline "Ready to Make History." Of course the other news organizations were not happy about the arrangement, but they honored the agreement, and the constant hounding by reporters of the Mercury Seven and their families died down.

The same day as the issue of *Life* Magazine hit the stands, the Soviet Union made space history of its own. On September 13 the Soviets had launched a rocket into space carrying a spherical spacecraft called Luna 2. But unlike previous Soviet launches, Luna 2 was not destined to orbit the earth; rather it was headed for the moon. After the third stage of the rocket separated, it headed directly for the lunar surface. Thirty-three and a half hours after lifting off from Earth, radio signals from Luna 2 abruptly ceased, indicating that the craft had crashed onto the surface of the moon, but not before it had radioed back all sorts of important information about space.

Once again America was stunned by the Soviet's achievements in space. The space race between the United States and the Russians was heating up. The achievement particularly galled Alan, who found it hard to look up at night and know that a Soviet spacecraft was lying on the surface of the moon. To make matters worse, Soviet president Nikita Khrushchev taunted that America now slept under a Soviet moon. It seemed to Alan and the rest of the Mercury Seven that the eyes of the free world were looking to them and NASA to restore their faith in the supremacy of the democratic system. Simply put, no matter the risk, the United States had to make a bold move in space, and soon.

Chapter 12

Delays and Disappointments

A lan Shepard stared nervously at the clock. For once he did not care whether the other six astronauts knew that he was anxious. They *all* were. It was five fifteen in the afternoon on Thursday, January 19, 1961, the eve of newly elected president John F. Kennedy's inauguration. More important to the men in the room, it was just minutes away from the announcement of the selection of the first American to be launched into space.

All seven of the astronauts had trained hard and were mentally and physically prepared for the challenge. Yet, as they all knew, in the end only one of them would get to be the first to ride in the Mercury capsule atop a Redstone rocket and be propelled out of the earth's atmosphere into space.

A few nerve-racking minutes later, Robert Gilruth, Director of NASA's Space Task Group, strolled into the Mercury astronauts' office at Langley. He cleared his throat. "What I'm about to announce is the most difficult decision I've ever had to make," he said grimly. "It is essential that the decision be known to only a small group of people. We'll make it known to the public at the appropriate time."

This was not new to Alan. He had expected the decision to be kept confidential, at least for a while.

Robert Gilruth looked up and without further ado said, "Alan Shepard will make the first suborbital Redstone flight. Gus Grissom will follow Alan on the second suborbital flight. John Glenn will be the backup for both missions."

Alan immediately looked down. This was not the time for his trademark wide grin. Everyone in the room had fought hard to be the first man in space, and he was now in the presence of six very disappointed colleagues.

"Are there any questions?" Gilruth asked.

No one said a word.

"Thank you very much, and good luck," he said as he turned and walked out of the office, leaving the Mercury Seven alone.

After a short silence, John Glenn walked over and shook Alan's hand, and one by one the other men followed his lead. Then they all filed out the door. No one apparently felt like toasting Alan's good fortune. When the last man had left, Alan let out a whoop and headed for the door and for home.

When he arrived home, Alan raced into the house, threw his arms around Louise, and blurted, "Lady, you can't tell anyone, but you have your arms around the man who'll be first in space!"

Louise laughed. "You got it! You got the first ride?"

Alan hugged her harder. It was the culmination of many years of sacrifice for both of them.

The following morning Alan and Louise rose early, loaded their three daughters into the car, and set out for Washington, D.C., to watch the presidential mantle of the United States be passed from the country's oldest president, Dwight Eisenhower, to its youngest, John F. Kennedy.

Heavy snow was falling as the family took their places among the huge crowd that had gathered for the inauguration. John F. Kennedy, dressed in a top hat and tails, took the presidential oath of office, and then everyone settled in as he made his way to the podium and began delivering his inaugural speech.

As the new president spoke, Alan listened intently, nodding in agreement from time to time, especially as Kennedy addressed the Cold War that existed between the United States and the Soviet Union.

Finally, to those nations who would make themselves our adversary, we offer not a pledge but a request: that both sides begin anew the quest for peace, before the dark powers of destruction unleashed by science engulf all humanity in planned or accidental self-destruction.

We dare not tempt them with weakness. For only when our arms are sufficient beyond doubt can we be certain beyond doubt that they will never be employed.

But neither can two great and powerful groups of nations take comfort from our present course—both sides overburdened by the cost of modern weapons, both rightly alarmed by the steady spread of the deadly atom, yet both racing to alter that uncertain balance of terror that stays the hand of mankind's final war.

So let us begin anew, remembering on both sides that civility is not a sign of weakness, and sincerity is always subject to proof. Let us never negotiate out of fear, but let us never fear to negotiate.

Let both sides explore what problems unite us instead of belaboring those problems which divide us.

Let both sides, for the first time, formulate serious and precise proposals for the inspection and control of arms, and bring the absolute power to destroy other nations under the absolute control of all nations.

Let both sides seek to invoke the wonders of science instead of its terrors. Together let us explore the stars, conquer the deserts, eradicate disease, tap the ocean depths, and encourage the arts and commerce.

Let both sides unite to heed, in all cor-
ners of the earth, the command of Isaiah to
"undo the heavy burdens, and [to] let the
oppressed go free." And, if a beachhead of
cooperation may push back the jungle of
suspicion, let both sides join in creating a
new endeavor—not a new balance of power,
but a new world of law—where the strong
are just, and the weak secure, and the peace
preserved. All this will not be finished in the
first one hundred days. Nor will it be finished in the first one thousand days; nor in
the life of this administration; nor even perhaps in our lifetime on this planet. But let us
begin. In your hands, my fellow citizens,
more than mine, will rest the final success or
failure of our course....

Can we forge against these enemies a
grand and global alliance, North and South,
East and West, that can assure a more fruit-
ful life for all mankind? Will you join in that
historic effort? In the long history of the
world, only a few generations have been
granted the role of defending freedom in its
hour of maximum danger. I do not shrink
from this responsibility—I welcome it. I do
not believe that any of us would exchange
places with any other people or any other
generation. The energy, the faith, the devo-
tion which we bring to this endeavor will
light our country and all who serve it. And
the glow from that fire can truly light the

world. And so, my fellow Americans, ask not what your country can do for you; ask what you can do for your country.

Alan felt the personal weight of President Kennedy's last remark. Although the public did not yet know it, he knew exactly what he could do for his country: pioneer manned spaceflight and show the world that the Soviets did not have the technological edge over the United States.

The planned launch date for Alan's flight to space was only two months away, and a lot of work had to be done before then. NASA wanted to launch one last Redstone rocket with a chimpanzee aboard before it sent a human into space. On January 31, 1961, a Redstone rocket blasted into space from Cape Canaveral. Strapped into the Mercury capsule that sat atop the rocket was a thirty-seven-pound chimpanzee named Ham. The purpose of the test flight was twofold, to test the Redstone rocket one last time before it was used to blast Alan into space and to test the communication system between the ground controllers and the Mercury capsule in space. To do this, Ham had been trained to pull a certain lever when signaled to from the ground. If he carried out the command correctly, he would be automatically rewarded with a banana pellet. And if he failed to follow the command, he would receive a low-voltage electric shock through his feet.

Things did not go well with the flight. At first the lever reward system performed flawlessly, and Ham received his banana pellets for pulling the lever when commanded to do so. But then something went wrong with the capsule's electrical system so that instead of receiving the pellets for a reward, no matter what Ham did, he continually received an electric shock. As well, a faulty valve in the rocket caused too much fuel to be delivered to the engine, causing the Redstone to fly faster and higher than intended. And since the rocket burned its fuel faster than planned, its fuel tank ran dry, causing the capsule to make an emergency separation. This, in turn, led to the capsule's reentering the earth's atmosphere too fast and at the wrong angle. And the heat buildup from reentry caused the temperature inside the capsule to soar, while Ham experienced twice as many g-forces as planned. To top things off, when the capsule finally splashed down into the Atlantic Ocean, it sprung a leak and began to fill with water. When the recovery crew finally reached the sinking capsule, Ham had survived the perilous journey. But he was not a happy chimpanzee, and he tried to bite his rescuers.

Ham's unfortunate experience had unforeseen repercussions for the plan to put a man in space. While NASA categorized the test flight as a success—after all, Ham had returned to Earth alive, if a little upset—Wernher von Braun was not happy with the result and wanted another test flight of the Redstone rocket with a chimpanzee aboard. Even when the NASA engineers confirmed that the source of the problem was a faulty electrical relay that could easily be replaced, von Braun was not ready to move on.

Alan was furious at this decision. *If he was willing to risk his life, why shouldn't he be on the next rocket,* he fumed. He did everything in his power to try to change the decision but was told by Chris Kraft, NASA's flight director, that when it came to rockets, von Braun was king, and if the king wanted another test flight, there would be another test flight.

It galled Alan when the March 24 Redstone test flight, complete with a chimpanzee in the Mercury capsule, went flawlessly. Alan would have given anything to have been the one strapped into that seat. Instead he was on the ground watching the flight. He just hoped it would not be too long before he got his chance to be the first man in space.

Nearly three weeks later, early in the morning of April 12, 1961, the ringing of the telephone beside his bed awoke Alan from a deep sleep in a hotel room near Cape Canaveral. Groggily he reached over and picked up the phone. "What?" he demanded, annoyed at being awakened in the early hours of the morning. Surely whoever it was could have waited until the sun was up.

"Commander Shepard?" Alan recognized the voice of a NASA engineer.

"Yeah, this is Shepard," Alan said, still puzzled as to what could be so important that he had to be awakened in the middle of the night.

"Have you heard?" the engineer asked.

"Heard what?" Alan replied.

"The Russians have put a man in orbit."

Alan was suddenly wide awake. He sat bolt upright. "They what?" he asked.

"The Russians put a man in orbit," the engineer repeated.

"You've got to be kidding me," Alan snapped.

"I wouldn't do that, Commander. They've really done it. They've put a man in space."

Alan thanked the engineer for the news and hung up the phone. He sat staring blankly at the wall, trying to grapple with the news. He wouldn't be the first man in space, after all. Slowly anger and frustration overcame him. He slammed his fist down on the bedside table and fumed, *I could have beaten the Soviets, if von Braun had not been such a wimp. Now we'll spend years playing catch-up.*

When the sun finally came up that morning, things got worse. Newspapers all over the United States blared the headline,

SOVIETS SEND MAN INTO SPACE
SPOKESMAN SAYS U.S. ASLEEP

Alan quickly read the details of the Soviet's manned flight. At 9:07 AM Moscow time, a huge Russian SS-6 rocket had blasted off the launchpad. Atop the rocket sat a five-ton Vostok spacecraft named *Swallow,* and strapped inside the spacecraft was a twenty-seven-year-old Russian cosmonaut named Yuri Gagarin. The rocket had blasted him 112 miles above the earth, where *Swallow* separated from the third stage of the rocket and made an elliptical orbit of the earth, taking Gagarin to a distance of 203 miles above Earth at its apex. It took *Swallow* eighty-nine minutes to orbit the earth, and then retrorockets had fired and set the spacecraft on a trajectory to reenter the atmosphere.

Finally the craft had drifted down to Earth and landed in a field beside the Volga River, where Yuri Gagarin had been safely recovered.

Alan was devastated by the news, as were millions of other Americans. The pride they felt in their country had been badly bruised, and many people began to ask, why bother being the second nation to put a man into space? Perhaps, they argued, the United States should admit that it had been beaten and put its money into more pressing issues at home.

Such an argument rattled the Mercury Seven, who held their breath as they waited to see how President Kennedy would react to the situation. At first Kennedy seemed resigned to giving up the space race, and he was encouraged in this resolve by Jerome Weisner, the head of the president's Science Advisory Committee. Weisner wanted President Kennedy to cancel the Mercury program before it became a laughingstock.

To make matters worse, on April 17, five days after Gagarin's successful orbit of the earth, an attempted invasion of Communist Cuba by Cuban exiles took place. President Kennedy had inherited the plan from the Eisenhower administration, but things did not go well. As the invading exiles stormed ashore at the Bay of Pigs on the southern shore of the island of Cuba, the promised American air cover did not materialize. President Kennedy, it seemed, was unsure of the invasion plan and at the last minute ordered American airplanes waiting to take off in support of the ground troops to stand

down. This allowed Fidel Castro's army to resound-
ingly defeat the ground invaders.

As a result of the abortive Bay of Pigs invasion,
public confidence in the White House and the
Kennedy administration plummeted. Obviously
President Kennedy needed to do something drastic
to bolster the country's flagging morale and redirect
the attention of the American people. He made an
announcement to the nation: the Mercury Project
would go ahead, with a manned spaceflight planned
for May 2.

Alan grinned when he heard the news. The space
race was back on.

Chapter 13

Light This Candle!

It was 5:00 AM Friday, May 5, 1961, and Alan Shepard stood staring up at the Redstone rocket on the launchpad at Cape Canaveral. It had stopped raining the night before, and he had finally been given clearance for liftoff. The launch attempt three days before on May 2 had had to be scrubbed because of bad weather. But today seemed to be a better day to head into space.

As Alan looked up at the "bird" with its black and white checkerboard painted top, he tried to control his emotions, but it was difficult. Dressed in his space suit and carrying his oxygen supply, he had planned to say a few words of thanks to the rocket crew standing nearby. But now, just moments before he was to take the elevator up to the Mercury capsule, he was too choked up to speak. Instead, he waved and stepped into the elevator. A minute later the elevator door opened onto the gantry, seventy feet above. John Glenn, dressed in white coveralls, helped Alan out of the elevator and then through the two-foot square opening into *Freedom 7*, the name Alan had chosen for the Mercury capsule. It was a maneuver the two men had practiced endlessly. Yet this morning Alan's suit seemed tighter than normal, and Alan was especially careful not to catch its silver fabric on any of the knobs and levels inside the capsule.

If the flight went ahead, Alan knew there were only two ways he would ever again exit that hatch. One was if the mission was successful, in which case he would land in the Atlantic Ocean somewhere north of the Bahamas and be picked up by a navy ship. The other was if the flight had to be aborted, in which case he was supposed to clip on a chest parachute, open the hatch, jump clear of the capsule, and float back to Earth. The chances of the second operation going well were almost zero, but Alan knew that NASA had included the parachute so that it could tell the media it had provided a personal means of escape if he needed it.

As Alan sat waiting for the NASA engineers to complete their preflight procedures and secure the capsule door from the outside, he thought about the news media. The media were the one thing none of the seven astronauts had taken into account when they volunteered for Project Mercury, and they were the single thing that seemed to dominate the way things were done. Alan supposed that NASA was right in one way: the *Freedom 7* flight, successful or not, had cost four hundred million dollars of taxpayers' money—over two dollars for every man, woman, and child in the United States. And now the people wanted to see a "show" that would make them proud to be Americans once again. The advent of television had made it possible for forty-five million Americans to watch the event live. This was a far different approach from the Soviet's manned spaceflight twenty-three days before, when everything had been kept top secret until the flight was over.

Alan imagined Louise and the girls huddled around the new TV at home in Virginia Beach. He knew that a hundred or more reporters, photographers, and television crew members would be spilled out into the street in front of the house waiting for the launch—and waiting to hear whether he lifted off safely or was blown to oblivion. If it was the latter, he knew they would eagerly record Louise's reaction to the death of her husband as she watched it on national TV.

An hour passed, and then John Glenn's smiling face broke into Alan's thoughts. "Time to lock you down," John said, thrusting his hand into the capsule. "See you soon. Happy landings, Commander!"

Alan reached out and shook John's hand, and then John pulled his arm out of the capsule. Alan could hear the rest of the gantry crew cheering as the hatch cover closed with a thud. He was now alone in his tiny spacecraft. It was time to concentrate on the 127 buttons and switches on the control panel in front of him.

Methodically Alan began going through the pre-liftoff procedures, trying to calm the butterflies in the pit of his stomach. As he ran through the check, he communicated over the radio with Gordon Cooper, situated in the blockhouse a short distance from the launchpad.

The Mercury capsule had two small portholes, one located off Alan's left shoulder and the other to his lower right, but from his strapped-in position, the portholes were both hard for him to see out of. Alan's main view of the outside world was through a periscope that had a fisheye lens mounted on it. The lens provided an ultrawide but distorted view as the image was displayed on a screen in front of Alan. Still, through the periscope Alan could see the gantry that surrounded the rocket being rolled away.

The countdown was suspended again at 7:14 AM, when clouds rolled in. For another half hour everyone waited for the weather to clear. During the half-hour hold, a problem developed with the rocket, and an electrical inverter had to be replaced. After fifty-two minutes, the countdown resumed, but after twenty-one minutes, it was again stopped when engineers discovered a computer error that had to be fixed before the rocket could fly.

Inside *Freedom 7* Alan began to get frustrated with all the holdups. He was ready to blast off. He could feel the adrenaline rushing through him. His heart was racing, and with each delay the butterflies crept back into the pit of his stomach. He found himself talking to himself, telling himself to calm down and relax.

And then Alan felt the worst of all feelings, at least for a man strapped into a spacecraft atop a rocket. He felt his bladder begin to throb. Alan needed to urinate. Of course by now the flight was supposed to have been over, and no one had thought it necessary to equip him with a urine collection system.

Alan explained his predicament over the radio to Gordon Cooper and asked if the gantry could be rolled back so that he could exit the capsule and relieve himself. Gordon radioed him back moments later to tell him that Wernher von Braun had said absolutely not; he would have to stay strapped into the capsule. But Alan really had to go, and he suggested that he urinate in his space suit. Gordon again radioed him back and told him that the flight surgeon forbade him to do that, as it would short out the electrical sensors attached all over his body. Then Alan came up with a solution. "Have them cut the power to the sensors while I pee," he told Gordon. Moments later Gordon radioed back. "Okay, go ahead and pee," he told Alan.

That is just what Alan did. Fortunately the bulky cotton underwear he was wearing absorbed the liquid, and the pure oxygen supply inside his space suit soon evaporated it, leaving Alan feeling dry.

As the holdups to launch mounted, Alan noticed agitation rising in the voices of controllers on the ground. Finally he barked over the radio to

Gordon, "I've been in here more than three hours. I'm a heck of a lot cooler than you guys. Why don't you just fix your little problem and light this candle!"

Soon all the problems were fixed, and the countdown began again.

Two minutes before liftoff, Alan heard the voice of Deke Slayton on the radio. Deke and Alan had become friends during their astronaut training, and the sound of his friend's voice had a comforting and calming effect on him. Deke was located at Mercury Control, two miles from the launchpad, and he would be capsule communicator, or "cap com," for the duration of Alan's flight.

At 9:32 AM Alan heard Deke begin the final countdown. Ten...Nine...Eight...Seven...Six... Alan gripped the abort handle tightly and braced his feet against the capsule floor. Five...Four...Three... *Don't screw up, Shepard,* he muttered to himself. Two...One...Zero...Ignition...

Alan could hear a rumble below him that began to grow like thunder. Then he heard Deke's voice on the radio say, "Liftoff."

Alan felt himself slowly, gently rising into the sky. Then the Redstone began to pick up speed.

"You're on your way!" Deke said excitedly.

"Roger. Liftoff, and the clock has started," Alan replied.

As the rocket began to climb, Alan started to reel off information over the radio to ground control. "This is *Freedom 7.* The fuel is go. 1.2 g. Cabin at 14 psi. Oxygen is go. Main buss is twenty-four, and the isolated battery is twenty-nine."

"Roger," Deke said.

Suddenly the smooth flight began to get rough, and the capsule rattled and shook violently. Alan's head hammered against his headrest, and he shook so much that he couldn't focus on the instrument panel in front of him. He was at the point where the rocket was about to pass through the sound barrier and reach supersonic speed. It was the point in the flight where the greatest stress was on the spacecraft. Alan tried to hold his head steady, but it was a hopeless task. And then suddenly he was through the sound barrier, and the bumpy ride faded away.

The Redstone roared on, higher and faster. Two minutes into the flight Alan was experiencing six g's as the craft accelerated. This meant that his body felt like it weighed a thousand pounds. But his training in the centrifuge, learning to deal with the increased weight of gravity, paid off. Alan was able to move his arms and continue to read off flight information to ground control.

Two minutes and 21.8 seconds after blasting off from Cape Canaveral, right on schedule, the Redstone's engine shut down. Less than a second later the escape tower attached to the nose of the capsule separated from the craft. The escape tower was no longer needed and would tumble back toward earth, burning up in the atmosphere as it did so.

Alan waited anxiously to see whether the Mercury capsule would separate from the spent rocket. Suddenly he felt three small rockets at the base of the capsule fire. *Freedom 7* lurched forward, and a green light on the control panel lit up, indicating that the capsule had separated from the Redstone rocket. Everything was going perfectly to plan.

"This is *Freedom 7*. Cap sep is green," he relayed to ground control.

"Roger," came the familiar voice of Deke over Alan's radio.

The autopilot system then rotated the Mercury capsule 180 degrees so that it was flying with its blunt end forward. At the same time, Alan began to experience the weightlessness of space. Moments before, he had felt like he weighed a thousand pounds. Now he felt like he weighed nothing. His body floated up from his seat and pressed against his restraints. Particles of dust floated in front of him, as did a washer, inadvertently left behind a control panel when the capsule was built.

For a moment Alan marveled at the sensation of actually being in space flying at a speed of 5,100 miles per hour. And then it was time to manually fly *Freedom 7*. When Yuri Gagarin was blasted into space by the Soviets, he had basically been a passenger in the spacecraft as it orbited the earth. The flying was done by the autopilot system, guided by controllers on the ground. To differentiate this flight from Gagarin's flight, it had been decided that Alan would take control of the Mercury capsule and manually fly it. Alan placed his hand on a control lever, exactly like the one he had used to control the MASTIF back in Cleveland. He then turned off the autopilot and took control of the capsule one axis at a time, first pitch, then yaw, and finally roll. As he moved the control lever, tiny jets on the outside of the craft would fire, moving the capsule in the same direction that he moved the particular control lever. Alan might not be the first man in space, but he was the first man to manually fly a spacecraft in space.

As he flew the capsule, Alan did his best to peer out the small portholes at the earth below. He also used the periscope, although he soon discovered that he had forgotten to remove a filter he'd put over the screen to diffuse the bright morning sunlight while he was stuck on the launchpad, and now he was unable to remove it. So while the view he saw through the periscope was spectacular, the vibrant colors of the earth from above were muted. Nonetheless, he was able to see the outline of the west coast of Florida and the Gulf of Mexico. Lake Okeechobee in central Florida was also visible, as were a number of the islands of the Bahamas.

At five minutes and fifteen seconds into the flight, shortly after *Freedom 7* reached the apogee of the arch it was following across the sky, at a height of 116.5 miles above the ground, three retrorockets fired as the spacecraft began its descent to Earth. Alan carefully guided the capsule to the correct angle for reentering the atmosphere and then retracted the periscope. At 7 minutes and 48.2 seconds after liftoff, a light on the control panel came on, indicating that the capsule had begun to reenter the atmosphere. Alan prepared for the full force of gravity. Soon he had gone from weightlessness to experiencing 11.6 g's on his body. Outside, the heat from friction with air molecules pushed the temperature of the heat shield to 1,200 degrees Fahrenheit, while the temperature inside the capsule rose to 102 degrees. Inside Alan's sealed space suit the temperature was 85 degrees.

Finally, at an altitude of twenty-one thousand feet, Alan felt the first parachute deploy. At fifteen thousand feet, a valve opened on the capsule to equalize cabin pressure with the outside air, and then at ten thousand feet, the main parachute deployed and carried *Freedom 7* down toward the water of the Atlantic Ocean at a rate of thirty feet per second. Fifteen minutes and twenty-two seconds after lifting off from Cape Canaveral, *Freedom 7* splashed down in the Atlantic, 302 miles east of the Cape and 100 miles north of the Bahamas.

Alan Shepard was back on Earth! And what an exhilarating ride it had been! Alan let out a whoop. Two minutes later he heard the sound of helicopter rotors beating the air above him. The crew of the helicopter attached a line to the capsule, and then Alan opened the hatch, crawled out, and grabbed the rescue collar that dangled from the helicopter. He pulled the collar over his head, secured it under his arms, and was slowly winched upward and in through the open door of the helicopter.

Grinning from ear to ear, Alan greeted his rescuers. The helicopter lifted *Freedom 7* out of the ocean and then headed for the nearby aircraft carrier USS *Lake Champlain.* Alan could scarcely believe the welcome that awaited him. Hundreds of white-capped sailors stood cheering on the vessel's deck. The capsule was lowered to the deck, and then the helicopter landed. As Alan climbed out of the helicopter a huge cheer went up from the crew of the *Lake Champlain*.

Once Alan was on the aircraft carrier, NASA doctors aboard ship whisked him away to check him out. After poking and prodding him, the doctors declared him to be fine. Alan could have told them that he had never felt better in his life.

After the medical checkout, Alan was given a tape recorder on which to record everything he could recall about his flight. And Alan had plenty to talk about.

Midway through recording his monologue on the tape recorder, Alan was interrupted by a phone call from Washington, D.C. Alan placed the phone to his ear. "Hello, Commander," he heard the voice on the other end of the line say, and he recognized it immediately as the voice of President Kennedy.

"Yes, sir," Alan replied.

"I want to congratulate you," the president said.

"Thank you very much, Mr. President."

"We watched you on TV, of course, and we are awfully proud of what you did."

"Thank you, sir," Alan said. "And as you know by now, everything worked out just perfectly."

And it had. No matter how many more tests they conducted on Alan over the next forty-eight hours, NASA doctors could not find any effect on his health from his time in space, except for his elated mood.

To add to that elation, two days later, a military helicopter carrying Alan and Louise Shepard touched down on the grounds of the White House in Washington, D.C. Standing by to greet them where they landed were President and Mrs. Kennedy. Alan and the president shook hands warmly, and then they all strolled toward the Rose Garden, where crowds of members of Congress and government officials thronged around them, cheering and yelling greetings to the first American in space.

The other members of the Mercury Seven were already waiting in front of a wooden platform in the Rose Garden. President Kennedy invited Alan onto the platform with him as television cameras whirled.

"Ladies and gentlemen," President Kennedy said, speaking into a microphone. "I want to express on behalf of us all the great pleasure we have in welcoming Commander Shepard and Mrs. Shepard here today. I think they know as citizens of this great country how proud we are of him, what satisfaction we have in his accomplishments, what a service he has rendered to our country."

After a few more remarks, President Kennedy turned to present Alan with the NASA Distinguished Service Medal. As he did so, the medal slipped out of his hands and fell onto the platform. The president and Alan both bent over to recover it and nearly bumped heads. President Kennedy picked up the medal and smiled. "This decoration has gone from the ground up!" he declared as he pinned it on Alan. The crowd went wild.

Following the ceremony in the Rose Garden, a presidential aide ushered the astronauts' wives off for a tour of the White House with Jackie Kennedy, while the president beckoned for Alan and the other astronauts and NASA officials to follow him. A few moments later they were all crowded into the Oval Office, along with Vice President Lyndon Johnson and several White House staff members. President Kennedy cleared his throat and asked a few general questions about what NASA was doing. Alan expected that, but he certainly did not expect what followed.

"I want a briefing," the president said, looking at NASA's Bob Gilruth.

As Alan listened to the president and Gilruth talk, he struggled to comprehend the continuing conversation. It was not about the next Redstone rocket, nor an orbital flight, the obvious next step. Suddenly Alan realized what the president and Gilruth were talking about—they were planning to put an American on the moon!

Later that day, Alan and Louise sat side by side in the lead limousine of a parade that made its way from the White House down Pennsylvania Avenue to the U.S. Capitol. A quarter of a million cheering, waving people lined the parade route, but Alan hardly noticed them. Only one thing reverberated in his mind: *was President Kennedy really serious about sending a man to the moon?*

Chapter 14

On to the Moon

On May 25, 1961, three weeks after his flight on *Freedom 7*, Alan Shepard and some of the other Mercury Seven astronauts sat in their office at the Langley, leaning in to hear the voice of President Kennedy on the radio. The president was addressing a special joint session of Congress.

> Mr. Speaker, Mr. Vice President, my copartners in government, gentlemen, and ladies: the Constitution imposes upon me the obligation to "from time to time give to the Congress information of the State of the Union." While this has traditionally been interpreted as an annual affair, this tradition has been broken in extraordinary times. These are extraordinary times. And we face an extraordinary challenge.

The president went on to talk about worldwide
social issues and the defense of the United States
at home and abroad. He then turned his attention
to the topic Alan and the others in the room had
been waiting for—the space race. The astronauts
listened intently to the president's words.

Finally, if we are to win the battle that is now
going on around the world between freedom
and tyranny, the dramatic achievements in
space which occurred in recent weeks
should have made clear to us all, as did the
Sputnik in 1957, the impact of this adventure on the minds of men everywhere, who
are attempting to make a determination of
which road they should take. Since early in
my term, our efforts in space have been
under review. With the advice of the Vice
President, who is Chairman of the National
Space Council, we have examined where we
are strong and where we are not, where we
may succeed and where we may not. Now it
is time to take longer strides—time for a
great new American enterprise—time for this
nation to take a clearly leading role in space
achievement, which in many ways may hold
the key to our future on earth.

I believe we possess all the resources and
talents necessary. But the facts of the matter
are that we have never made the national
decisions or marshaled the national resources required for such leadership. We

have never specified long-range goals on an
urgent time schedule, or managed our
resources and our time so as to ensure their
fulfillment.

Recognizing the head start obtained by
the Soviets with their large rocket engines,
which gives them many months of lead-time,
and recognizing the likelihood that they will
exploit this lead for some time to come in
still more impressive successes, we never-
theless are required to make new efforts on
our own. For while we cannot guarantee that
we shall one day be first, we can guarantee
that any failure to make this effort will make
us last. We take an additional risk by making it in full view of the world, but as shown
by the feat of astronaut Shepard, this very
risk enhances our stature when we are
successful.

But this is not merely a race. Space is
open to us now, and our eagerness to share
its meaning is not governed by the efforts of
others. We go into space because whatever
mankind must undertake, free men must
fully share.

I therefore ask the Congress, above and
beyond the increases I have earlier requested
for space activities, to provide the funds
which are needed to meet the following
national goals:

First, I believe that this nation should
commit itself to achieving the goal, before

this decade is out, of landing a man on the moon and returning him safely to the earth. No single space project in this period will be more impressive to mankind, or more important for the long-range exploration of space; and none will be so difficult or expensive to accomplish. We propose to accelerate the development of the appropriate lunar space-craft. We propose to develop alternate liquid and solid fuel boosters, much larger than any now being developed, until certain which is superior. We propose additional funds for other engine development and for unmanned explorations—explorations which are particularly important for one purpose which this nation will never overlook: the survival of the man who first makes this daring flight. But in a very real sense, it will not be one man going to the moon. If we make this judgment affirmatively, it will be an entire nation. For all of us must work to put him there.

The hairs on the back of Alan's neck rose as he listened to President Kennedy's words. Then he turned to Deke Slayton and asked, "Did I hear what I thought I heard?"

Deke nodded. "You heard right. The man wants to send us to land on the moon. *Land*, not just fly around the moon!"

The room filled with a stunned silence, and Alan was sure the others were all thinking the same thing: *the president wants one of us, someone right here in this room, to be the first human to walk on the moon and carry the hopes and dreams of the entire United States with him.*

Alan took a deep breath. He knew that the technology did not yet exist to get a man to the moon and back. There would be a lot of work ahead.

None of the Mercury Seven talked about anything else for days as they digested the news and tried to imagine how getting to the surface of the moon would become a reality. It seemed so fantastic, so far-fetched, yet they needed to act as if they had every confidence that it could be done.

Everyone's confidence, however, was shaken by the next Project Mercury flight. On July 21, Gus Grissom in *Liberty Bell 7* blasted off from Cape Canaveral atop a Redstone rocket. His flight went flawlessly and followed almost the exact same path as Alan's flight. However, things went awry after *Liberty Bell 7* splashed down in the Atlantic Ocean. Unlike *Freedom 7,* where Alan had to manually open the capsule's hatch cover, the hatch of Gus's Mercury capsule was rigged to open with an explosive charge. Soon after splashdown, the hatch cover on *Liberty Bell 7* exploded prematurely, and the capsule began to fill with water and sink. Gus managed to scramble out and swim away, but his space suit began to fill with water. A helicopter plucked Gus from the Atlantic Ocean only moments before he went under. It was a sober reminder to Alan and the other astronauts just how dangerous the endeavor they had undertaken was.

Despite the near mishap, later that same day, Congress voted to allot 1.8 billion dollars to the moon program, for which President Kennedy had already signed contracts with various manufacturers in many congressional districts around the country, ensuring widespread support of the program.

Sixteen days after Gus's flight in *Liberty Bell 7*, the Soviets struck again with the successful launch of *Vostok 2*. Aboard this spacecraft was cosmonaut Gherman Titov, who made seventeen and a half orbits of the earth, landing back in Russia the following day. The news had a riveting effect on Americans. It was time for the United States to step up to the plate.

NASA's original plan was for each of the Mercury Seven astronauts to complete one suborbital flight like Alan's before moving on to orbital flights. But with the Russians' latest space success, NASA had a change of heart. There wasn't time for the other five of the Mercury Seven astronauts to make suborbital space flights. The United States had to send a man up to orbit the earth, just as the Soviets had done, and President Kennedy wanted it done before the end of 1961. It was time to leave behind the underpowered Redstone rockets and enter the age of the Atlas rocket.

Alan was surprised when he heard of the decision to switch to the Atlas rocket. He recalled watching the failed launch of an Atlas D rocket at Cape Canaveral shortly after joining the Mercury Seven, and in testing to date, two out of every three

Atlas rockets exploded either at or just after liftoff. *These are not good odds,* he told himself.

NASA engineers were also aware of the problem, but if the president wanted an American astronaut to orbit the earth before the end of the year, they had no alternative but to switch to the Atlas rocket. The Atlas was the only rocket with the power to lift a Mercury capsule high enough so that it could attain orbit. NASA engineers thus put pressure on Convair, the company that manufactured the Atlas, to immediately fix the problems with the rocket or risk being fired by NASA.

Not wanting to lose their contract with NASA, Convair engineers got to work to make the Atlas stronger and to modify other systems that were causing problems. Their efforts seemed to pay off, and at a test launch on September 13, 1961, the modified Atlas rocket performed flawlessly, lifting an unmanned Mercury capsule aloft and putting it into orbit, where it circled the globe once before returning to earth. It was now time for a manned orbit of the earth in a Mercury capsule.

Much to his frustration, Alan was not chosen to be the first American to be put into orbit. That honor fell to John Glenn. Still, the Mercury Seven pulled together into a tight team around John, with Alan taking the lead role in understanding the complex ground operations that were needed to support a manned Mercury capsule in orbit.

Friendship 7, as John had decided to call his Mercury capsule, was scheduled to blast off into space on December 20 as an early Christmas gift for the citizens of the United States. However, one delay after another meant that it was not until February 20, 1962, that the Atlas rocket with John Glenn in *Friendship 7* atop it was ready for launch. At ten in the morning the Atlas rocket fired and lifted *Friendship 7* into the sky above Florida. The liftoff was perfect, and soon the Mercury capsule was placed into orbit.

Alan was in the Mercury Control Center during the flight, monitoring the spacecraft's performance on the dials and gauges on the console in front of him and listening to John describe the sight of the earth from space. During *Friendship 7*'s third and final orbit of earth, traveling at 17,500 miles per hour, three times the speed Alan had reached on his suborbital flight, a light began flashing a "segment 51" signal on Alan's console. Alan felt his heart skip a beat. The flashing light indicated that the bag behind the heat shield had deployed. The bag was supposed to deploy after the spacecraft had reentered the atmosphere, to cushion the impact when the capsule landed in the sea. But if the bag had deployed in space, before reentering the atmosphere, it would burn up on reentry and the heat shield would fall away, leaving John and *Friendship 7* to burn up. The problem was serious, and something had to be done about it—now!

Alan raced to tell Chris Kraft, NASA's flight director, of the problem. Chris told him that it could be a serious problem or just a faulty circuit in the capsule, and Alan had a hunch that it was the latter. Still they could take no chances. NASA engineers were summoned to start coming up with a solution, and Alan got on the phone with engineers at McDonnell Aircraft, the maker of the capsule.

Precious minutes passed as everyone talked over the problem, and finally a possible solution was reached. The Mercury capsule would soon fire retrorockets to slow it down and position it for reentry, after which the retrorockets would be jettisoned. But the retrorockets were mounted on the heat shield, and, the engineers reasoned, if they did not jettison them, perhaps the retrorockets would hold the heat shield in place during reentry. It was risky. Of all the scenarios of what could go wrong with the capsule in space, nobody had ever envisioned this one.

By now John had fired his retrorockets, and *Friendship 7* was over Texas, ready to reenter Earth's atmosphere. Alan raced to his station, contacted John on the radio, and told him not to jettison the retrorockets, explaining why. Alan noticed a nervous edge in the voice of his fellow astronaut as he replied over the radio. Alan stayed on the radio talking to John and trying to calm him as *Friendship 7* plunged into the atmosphere.

Then the plunging Mercury capsule reached the point where the heat buildup of reentry interfered with the radio signal and made communication with the craft from Mercury Control impossible. The control room fell silent. Alan waited anxiously, not sure whether he would see John again or whether John would be incinerated by the heat of reentry.

Four minutes and twenty-three tension-filled seconds passed until the time when *Friendship 7* should have emerged from the fireball of reentry and radio communication could be resumed.

"*Friendship 7*, this is Cape. Do you read? Over. *Friendship 7*, this is Cape. Do you read? Over," Alan said over the radio to John.

The only reply to the radio message was static.

"*Friendship 7*, this is Cape. Do you read? Over," Alan said again.

Still there was only the crackle of static in reply, and Alan began to fret that his fellow Mercury astronaut had indeed been incinerated on reentry. And then, suddenly, the radio burst to life. "Loud and clear. How me?" came John's voice.

Alan had had his share of differences with John during their astronaut training, but at that moment, the sound of John's voice was the sweetest thing he had heard in a long time.

"Reading you loud and clear. How do you feel?" Alan replied into the radio microphone.

"Pretty good," came John's reply.

Four hours and forty-three minutes after lifting off from Cape Canaveral, *Friendship 7* splashed down in the Atlantic Ocean, and John Glenn was plucked to safety by a helicopter.

Despite the unexpected scare with the heat shield, the mission had been a complete success. The United States had now orbited a man in space around the earth. And not only that, it had done the Soviets one better in the space race. Now three American astronauts had flown successfully in space compared to the two cosmonauts the Soviets had blasted aloft.

With one orbital flight successfully under its belt, NASA pushed for a second one. Just three months later, on May 24, 1962, Scott Carpenter became the fourth American in space. His flight aboard *Aurora 7* would turn out to be a harrowing experience for Alan, who served as cap com on the ground in California for the flight.

As he orbited Earth, Scott became entranced with the view from above. To get a better view of the world stretched before him, he constantly fired his retrorockets to maneuver the capsule. By the time he began his third and last orbit of the earth, his fuel tank was seriously low, and he still had to use his retrorockets to slow the capsule and position it for reentry. Alan warned him of the situation and told him not to needlessly use up any more of the precious fuel supply by firing the rockets.

Yet as he talked to Scott, Alan was perturbed. Scott seemed to be disoriented, more focused on the view than on the checklist of things he had to do before reentry. He began to fall behind schedule, and Alan got on the radio and began to talk him through what needed to be done for reentry. Scott would be attentive and follow Alan's instruction, but then he would lose focus and be overcome by the view again. Alan kept talking to him calmly, telling him what to do next. It reminded Alan of the time while serving on the USS *Oriskany* when his commander, Jig Dog, had become disoriented dur-ing a training exercise and risked crashing his plane into the sea. Then Alan had remained calm on the radio and talked Jig Dog through the crisis until he landed safely back on the carrier.

That is what Alan did with Scott. He continued talking to him in a calm but firm way. He counted down to the precise time Scott needed to fire his retrorocket to put him on course for reentry, but Scott was three seconds late doing this. Alan knew exactly what this mistake meant. If *Aurora 7* made it safely through the rigors of reentry, it would land well off course. It also meant that at that moment the spacecraft would not be properly lined up for reentry and could bounce off the earth's atmosphere and tumble off into space, leaving Scott stuck alive inside until his oxygen supply was depleted.

Alan quickly began relaying instructions to Scott, telling him when to fire his retrorockets to get his capsule onto the proper angle for reentry. He had no way of telling whether Scott had been able to do this before *Aurora 7* plunged into the atmosphere and entered the period where the heat buildup from reentry made it impossible to communicate with the spacecraft.

Alan, along with everyone else at Mission Control, waited anxiously for the four and a half minutes of radio silence to pass. When the time had passed, there was no radio communication with *Aurora 7*. Alan tried desperately to contact the capsule, but the radio channel from *Aurora 7* remained silent. After fifteen minutes, the time when the spacecraft should have splashed down, the radio was still silent, and the navy ships in the recovery zone could not pick up a signal from Scott's homing beacon. Alan hung his head and feared the worst: Scott had not been able to adjust his angle in time, and his Mercury capsule, with him inside, had been incinerated during reentry.

Forty minutes passed, and then Alan received the amazing news—Scott Carpenter was alive. *Aurora 7* had splashed down 250 miles off course and well outside radio beacon contact distance with the recovery ship. A Marine helicopter had eventually been able to get a fix on the capsule, and Scott was found floating in a life raft beside his spacecraft, eating a candy bar. Alan let out a sigh of relief. His cool handling of the stressful situation had saved Scott's life.

Alan soon learned, however, that Cris Kraft, NASA's flight director, was so furious with Scott's performance during the flight that he had permanently grounded Scott as an astronaut.

Despite the drama of the flight, it was deemed a success, and now only one more flight of the Mercury capsule remained. It was scheduled for May 1963, and Gordon Cooper was assigned to fly the capsule, which he named *Faith 7*.

After the successful flight of *Faith 7*, it was time for Project Gemini, a new project designed to allow astronauts in orbit to learn the new practices and maneuvers they would need to know if the United States were to land a man on the moon. These things included learning to handle long-duration spaceflight, walking in space, and rendezvousing and docking with another spacecraft. The new Gemini capsule, bigger than its Mercury predecessor, was designed to carry two men into space and allow them to stay aloft orbiting Earth for much longer periods of time.

In late 1963, Alan Shepard was chosen to be one of two astronauts to pilot the first Gemini flight. Tom Stafford, one of a new batch of astronaut recruits, dubbed by the press as the "Next Nine," would to go along with Alan on the flight.

While Project Gemini was ramping up, NASA was in the early planning stages of Project Apollo, which would finally land an American on the moon. Every time Alan peered up at the night sky as he prepared for his Gemini flight, he reminded himself that he was right on track—first astronaut on the Mercury mission, now first astronaut on the Gemini mission, and hopefully first man on the moon. However, something far beyond Alan's control intervened, throwing his life onto an entirely different trajectory.

Chapter 15

Grounded

Six weeks into his training for Project Gemini, Alan had to admit that something was wrong. Most of the time he was fine, but occasionally, and thankfully never in public, he had strange dizzy spells. They reminded him of the times he had been battered about, learning to master the MASTIF. But a mechanical beast was not bringing on these dizzy spells. From the best Alan could tell, they came from inside his body. Suddenly he would feel as if the world were spinning around him, and then he wouldn't know which way was up, or even where to reach out for a wall to steady himself. He'd fall to the ground, vomit, and then wait for things to return to normal. It occurred to him that he should not really be driving a car in such a state, much less piloting a spacecraft!

The dizzy spells would eventually go away, but they always came back. Alan finally decided to seek some medical help, not from a NASA doctor but from a private physician who was honor-bound not to reveal anything about Alan's condition to anyone, especially Alan's superiors at NASA.

The doctor was of little help, however. He prescribed a regimen of vitamins, which did nothing to improve Alan's condition. In fact, it continued to deteriorate, and Alan began to hear a ringing sound in his left ear.

It was one of the most difficult situations Alan had ever faced. Louise and the doctor knew what was going on, but Alan managed to keep his condition a secret from everyone else. Yet he knew that if he did make it back into space and had a dizzy spell while up there, he could well put his life and that of fellow astronaut Tom Stafford in jeopardy. Yet even with this knowledge, Alan could not bring himself to confide in the NASA doctors about his condition. He knew that if he did so, they would immediately ground him from further flights.

As fate would have it, Alan did not have to make that decision, because his illness was soon displayed for all to see. Alan was giving a lecture in Houston, Texas, the city to which he and Louise had recently moved when NASA's new Manned Spacecraft Center opened, when he felt the familiar dizzy sensation. Struggling to appear normal, Alan clutched the podium and stammered on. But the spinning got worse, and he shut his eyes. Next thing Alan knew, strong arms were guiding him off the stage and into a nearby chair. All around him cameras flashed. The game was up for him.

NASA's doctors quickly diagnosed Alan's condition as Ménière's disease, a little-understood illness that causes a buildup of fluid in the inner ear, the part of the body that helps to regulate balance. The doctors told Alan that they could do little for his condition, which had only a 20 percent chance of healing itself.

In the meantime Alan was grounded. Hearing this was one of the most difficult things Alan had ever had to deal with, especially since he had just turned forty and was wondering just how many more flights NASA would assign him.

Alan spent several weeks prowling around NASA's Manned Spacecraft Center like a lion with a thorn in his paw. His aggravation was so great that his fellow astronauts would take the stairs if he took the elevator, and secretaries would drop papers on his desk and scurry from his office before he had a chance to snap at them.

Finally Alan knew he had to face up to the reality of his situation. He decided to have a frank talk with Deke Slayton, who had faced a similar disappointment when NASA doctors discovered that he had a heart murmur. And even though the doctors concluded that the murmur did not affect his flying abilities in any way, NASA higher-ups had decided to pull Deke from the Mercury Seven team. Now Deke was the head of the astronaut office, and among his many duties was the task of selecting and overseeing the training of new astronauts. In fact, he had recently overseen the selection of a third group of fourteen astronauts who were now in training for Project Gemini and for Project Apollo that would follow it.

As Alan sat across the desk from Deke, he felt a new appreciation for what his friend had been through.

"Should I just hang it up? Or hang around here and hope for the best?" Alan shrugged. "The odds are eighty percent against me, and I can't keep going like this."

Deke smiled. "I have a job for you."

"What job?" Alan asked suspiciously.

"My job," Deke replied. "I've been made the chief of flight crew operations, and they're looking for someone to take my place here. How about it?"

"Any chance they'll let me up there again?" Alan asked, motioning upward with his head.

"I'm staying around for my chance, and your odds are better than mine," Deke said. "So what do you think about the new position?"

Alan sighed. It was not the life he wanted to live—he was born to fly—but at least he would still be around the astronaut program. And there was still a slim chance of one day getting another trip into space. Finally he nodded and reached out to shake Deke's hand.

In his new position as chief of the astronaut office, Alan was officially responsible for coordinating, scheduling, and controlling all activities that involved NASA astronauts. It was also his job to develop and implement effective training programs

for the astronauts and assign them to upcoming
manned space flights. His first assignment in the
new position was to oversee his replacement on the
upcoming manned Gemini mission, Gemini 3,
scheduled for launch on March 23, 1965. Gemini 1
and 2 had been unmanned test missions.

It was eventually decided that both Alan and
Tom Stafford would be replaced on the mission, and
Gus Grissom and another of the Next Nine astronauts, John Young, were named as their replace-
ments. It stretched Alan's emotions to the limit to
have to play a support role for a flight that would
have been his had it not been for Ménière's disease.

To make matters worse, morale was low at the
Manned Spacecraft Center in Houston as prepara-
tion and training got under way for the mission.
The year before, on November 22, 1963, President
John F. Kennedy had been shot and killed while
riding with his wife in a presidential motorcade
through the streets of Dallas, Texas. His assassination was a bitter blow to the entire country, but it
was particularly bitter for NASA which, with the
death of John F. Kennedy, lost its political patron
saint. The space program continued, but the new
president, Lyndon Johnson, did not have the same
charisma or vision for it as his predecessor, and
this in turn began to eat away at NASA's morale.

Meanwhile, the Soviets were streaking ahead in
the space race. On March 18, 1965, during the
flight of *Voskhod 2*, Aleksey Leonov, a lieutenant
colonel in the Soviet Air Force, became the first
man to leave a spacecraft in orbit and float in

space. Soviet newspapers carried stories of the feat and taunted America's space program. "The gap is not closing, but increasing. The so-called system of free enterprise is turning out to be powerless in competition with socialism in such a complex and modern area as space research," an article in the Russian newspaper *Pravda* declared.

The event was another galling and spectacular Soviet success in space, and it completely overshadowed the launch five days later of Gemini 3, with Gus Grissom and John Young aboard. Even though things with the first manned Gemini flight went well, it served to remind the American people how far ahead the Russians were in the space race.

Still, the Gemini program continued, and before 1965 drew to a close, four more successful Gemini missions had been completed. On Gemini 4, astronaut Ed White became the first American to walk in space; and the two astronauts aboard Gemini 7, Frank Borman and Jim Lovell, stayed in space orbiting the earth for almost fourteen days. During 1966, there were five more successful Gemini missions. Gemini 8 carried out the first successful docking with another vehicle in space, and this maneuver was perfected on subsequent flights. As well, Gemini 11 reached a record altitude of 739 miles in space.

Although Alan was closely involved with each of the Gemini missions, since he was no longer actively training as an astronaut, he had plenty of spare time in which to do other things. His mind turned to business, which was not surprising, given his father's and grandfather's business acumen. Before long Alan had quite a portfolio: he was vice president and part owner of a small bank, an investor in an oil-drilling operation, and a partner in a Texas cattle ranch.

Meanwhile, his Ménière's disease continued to bother him on and off, even though he tried every remedy the doctors suggested.

With the flight of Gemini 12 in November 1966, Project Gemini drew to a close. The project had been a great success. Astronauts flying in the various Gemini spacecraft had mastered many of the procedures and techniques they would need to employ to get to the moon. They also tested many of the components that would be needed to land a man on the moon and bring him safely back to Earth. In fact, although the start of Project Gemini had been overshadowed by Soviet achievements in space, by the time the project drew to a close, the United States was clearly ahead in the space race.

With the end of Gemini, it was time for NASA to focus all its resources on Project Apollo. Planning and development of the project had been going on in the background for years at NASA, but now it moved to center stage. A new rocket, the Saturn V, had been developed to lift the much heavier payloads of Apollo into space. This three-stage rocket, designed by Wernher von Braun, stood 363 feet tall, produced 7.8 million pounds of thrust at lift, and could carry a payload of 260,000 pounds into space. It was bigger and more powerful than any NASA had previously launched. As a result, a new launch facility was developed for it.

In 1961, NASA had acquired a huge tract of land on Merritt Island, located just across the Banana River from the Cape Canaveral Air Force Station, where rocket launches were carried out. On this land NASA had begun the development of a new facility called the Launch Operations Center, which, after the assassination of President Kennedy, was renamed Kennedy Space Center. From 1963 on, facilities at the new space center had quickly taken shape. Launchpads had been built, along with various operational support buildings, including the massive 525-foot-high Vehicle Assembly Building, which could easily house one of the new Saturn V rockets standing on end.

By the end of the Gemini program, everything at Kennedy Space Center was in place for Project Apollo. The Saturn V rocket had been tested and certified as ready for flight, and a new three-man capsule was being built. All that needed to be done now was to choose the astronauts who would fly on the early Project Apollo missions. Of the original Mercury Seven astronauts, only three were in contention to fly on Apollo. Alan and Deke Slayton had been grounded for medical reasons, as had John Glenn. In a strange coincidence, John had also been afflicted with an inner-ear/balance problem, though his condition stemmed from a bang he received to the head after slipping on a bathmat. In 1964 he left the astronaut program. Scott Carpenter was still grounded as a result of his performance during the *Aurora 7* flight. This left Gus Grissom,

Wally Schirra, and Gordon Cooper as the only three active astronauts from the Mercury Seven team.

Finally Gus Grissom was chosen to be the commander of Apollo 1, and accompanying him on the flight would be astronauts Ed White and Roger Chaffee. Of course Alan was bitterly disappointed that he would not be on the flight. More than anything else, he wanted to get back into space.

Building a spacecraft capable of carrying men to the moon and back was a complex task. After all, no one had ever built one before. The job turned out to be an incredible headache for engineers and astronauts alike. Nothing seemed to go right, resulting in delay after delay. Gus and Alan would often sit for hours behind closed doors, hashing over the details of the first Apollo mission. Gus made no secret of the fact that he thought the spacecraft was not yet ready to fly, and some NASA engineers agreed with him, calling the workmanship on the Apollo capsule "sloppy and unsafe."

Despite these concerns, NASA managers were feeling pressure to launch Apollo 1 as soon as possible. It was the mid-1960s, and the United States was in turmoil. The Vietnam War was in full swing, and things were not going well there for American soldiers, leading to open antiwar demonstrations at home. A growing civil rights movement further stirred the turmoil at home. It was a bleak time for the country. As a result, President Johnson decided that Americans needed something hopeful. And that something, he decided, was the Apollo project.

Finally, February 21, 1967, was chosen as the launch date for Apollo 1. The pressure was on NASA to fix the problems and get the spacecraft launched. Eventually everything was deemed to be ready, and on January 27, 1967, Gus Grissom, Roger Chaffee, and Ed White donned their space suits and headed for the launchpad for a dry run, a simulated liftoff of the spacecraft to check that all systems were working and Apollo 1 was ready to fly. As the three astronauts climbed aboard, the capsule was already mounted atop the Saturn rocket that would eventually lift it into space.

That day Alan was in Dallas, Texas, representing NASA at a dinner party. He had just stood to make a speech when someone came up beside him and whispered in his ear. "Sir," the person said, "there has been a terrible accident on Apollo 1. There were no survivors."

The blood drained from Alan's face at the news. Alan could scarcely believe it. He turned to the assembled crowd he was supposed to address and said, "I have just been informed of the loss...the loss of my comrades." With that he turned and left the room.

Alan headed straight for Houston, where he broke the news to Louise, who immediately left to be with Gus's wife, Betty, while Alan drove to the Manned Spacecraft Center, where he learned the details of the tragedy. There had been a fire inside the capsule, and none of the three astronauts had been able to escape in time. In the 100 percent oxygen environment inside Apollo 1, the fire had burned fast and furiously, killing the three astronauts in about seventeen seconds.

Alan did not sleep that night, or for many nights afterward. He thought about the good times he'd had with Gus as they trained together as part of the Mercury Seven. He also thought about the conversations with Gus regarding Apollo 1. He knew he could have done more to help Gus publicize the safety concerns he'd had about the Apollo spacecraft. And Alan felt even sadder and angrier when it was determined that the cause of the fire was a spark from faulty wiring under the seat, something that was completely preventable. As a result, he found himself supporting those who were calling for NASA to ground all flights for a year so that a complete review could be conducted of the agency's safety standards and practices.

In the wake of the disaster, NASA did decide to ground further Apollo flights until safety concerns could be addressed and design changes made to the capsule. The alterations included a change in the atmosphere inside the capsule at launch time. Instead of pure oxygen, the capsule would now be pressurized with sixty percent oxygen and forty percent nitrogen. In the twenty-four hours after liftoff, this mixture would slowly be changed to an atmosphere of pure oxygen. Also, the hatch door was changed to open outward and to open from the inside in less than ten seconds. As well, many of the flammable materials inside the capsule were replaced, and the wiring was covered with protective insulation. The space suits the astronauts would wear on all future missions were also changed. Gone were the nylon suits that burned easily, replaced by space suits made of a coated glass fabric that was difficult to set ablaze.

While changes were being made to the capsule, a number of unmanned Apollo test flights were launched to further test the Saturn V rocket.

Twenty months would pass before the redesigned Apollo space capsule was ready to fly again with astronauts aboard. Apollo 7, commanded by Wally Schirra, was scheduled to blast into space on October 11, 1968, where the three astronauts aboard would spend eleven days orbiting Earth. If this flight was a success, Apollo 8 would blast off from Kennedy Space Center on December 21, 1968, and head for the moon, which it would orbit for twenty hours.

Alan, of course, was kept busy helping the Apollo astronauts prepare for these upcoming missions. It seemed to him that this was what he would do until he finally decided to retire from NASA. It was a gloomy outlook for a man whose passion was to fly higher and faster than anyone else. And then one morning in the summer of 1968, a ray of hope shined into his life. Tom Stafford knocked on the door and walked into Alan's office. "Morning, boss," he said.

Alan put down his pen and smiled. "What's up?"

Tom looked unusually intense. "I've just heard about something you might be interested in. I have a friend who says he knows a surgeon in Los Angeles who is doing some pioneer work on curing

Ménière's disease. His name is Dr. William House, and I thought you might like to look into it."

"Sure," Alan replied, jotting down the doctor's name. "I'll have a talk with the guy." He tried to sound as casual as he could on the outside, but inside his hopes were soaring. In the nearly five years that he'd had the disease he had never heard of any kind of surgery to correct it.

As soon as Tom left his office, Alan was on the phone tracking down Dr. House. When he finally got to talk to him, the news was mixed. Yes, the doctor had performed six surgeries on patients with Ménière's disease, and some of those patients had been cured—but not all of them. In fact, the disease had worsened in some of them since the operation. The surgery was still experimental, and Dr. House could not predict which way a particular patient would respond to the treatment.

Despite these warnings, Alan's heart soared. This was the opportunity he had been waiting for. Sure it was a gamble, he reminded himself, but his whole career was a gamble. He could be killed in an accident at any time, just like Gus Grissom had been. Now, at least, he had a ray of hope. He arranged to meet with Dr. House as soon as possible for a preliminary assessment. Perhaps he would even be flying again by fall!

When they met, Dr. House explained the surgical procedure to Alan. He would drill through the mastoid bone behind the ear and insert a tiny tube that would drain the excess fluid that kept building up in the inner ear and redirect it into Alan's spinal column. It was a risky operation, but Alan was not deterred. He booked into St. Vincent's Hospital in Los Angeles under the name Victor Poulos, so as not to bring attention to himself, and hoped for the best.

The operation went smoothly, though Dr. House warned Alan after the surgery that it would be months before they knew for sure whether or not it had been a complete success. But Alan Shepard did not have months to wait. He hit the ground running. He assumed that he was 100 percent cured, and he wanted back into the astronaut program. Not only that, he was determined to fly to the moon!

Flight Status Restored

After the surgery in Los Angeles, Alan returned to Houston and his job as head of the astronaut office. His first stop after arriving back at work was Deke's office. As director of flight crew operations, Deke was the person Alan had to convince that he was cured of his Ménière's disease and was ready to fly again. Deke told Alan that he hoped his inner-ear problem had indeed been taken care of, but it was too early to know for sure or to pencil Alan in for a flight on Apollo. Still, Alan left Deke's office optimistic that he would eventually be back in space. He just had to convince everyone that he was cured and could safely fly.

Meanwhile, Apollo 7 blasted off on schedule on October 11, 1968, on its eleven-day mission orbiting the earth, where Wally Schirra and his crew tested all of the redesigned spacecraft's systems. Then on December 21, Apollo 8 blasted off. As planned, it headed for the moon, where it began orbiting. The three astronauts aboard were the first humans ever to see the far side of the moon. As they emerged from behind the moon, the crew sent Christmas greetings to earth, prayed for peace, and gave the first Bible reading from space. The astronauts quoted from Genesis 1: "In the beginning God created the heaven and earth." On Christmas Eve they radioed back riveting descriptions of the lunar surface as they orbited sixty miles above the moon. One of the astronauts, Frank Borman, also described the incredible sight of the blue and white earth rising above the moon's horizon. He called it the most beautiful sight he had ever seen.

The astronauts' description of the moon and the "earth rise," along with the pictures they took, captured the imagination of the American people. It also captured Alan's imagination as he saw himself one day soon standing on the surface of the moon looking back at the earth.

Apollo 9, followed in March 1969. The spacecraft orbited the earth for ten days, during which time the crew aboard docked with the lunar excursion module (LEM) stowed on top of the third stage of the Saturn V rocket. The buglike LEM was designed to carry two astronauts down to the surface of the moon and then carry them back to the Apollo capsule orbiting above. The crew of Apollo 9 successfully flew the LEM in space, testing its engines and maneuverability, before returning to Earth.

While all of this was going on around him, Alan was doing everything in his power to get back into space. He began a vigorous workout schedule and started putting in time in the Apollo flight simulator, teaching himself the skills he would need to have to fly on an Apollo mission to the moon. NASA's doctors closely scrutinized his progress. To make sure that his Ménière's disease was truly cured and to ensure that the small tube inserted in his inner ear would stand up to the rigors of space flight, the doctors put Alan through extensive tests in the centrifuge and on the MASTIF. Alan passed the tests, and the doctors eventually concurred that his Ménière's disease had indeed been cured. As a result, on May 7, 1969, eleven days before Apollo 10 was to blast into space, Alan Shepard's flight status with NASA was officially restored. Alan could scarcely contain his excitement.

After blasting off from Kennedy Space Center, Apollo 10, like Apollo 8, headed for the moon in a full dress rehearsal for Apollo 11, the mission that would actually land a man on the moon. Apollo 10 docked flawlessly with the lunar excursion module and then set out on its long journey to the moon. In orbit around the moon, Tom Stafford and Gene Cernan crawled into the LEM while John Young stayed behind to pilot the Apollo command module as it orbited the moon. Stafford and Cernan detached from the capsule and flew the LEM down to within eight and a half miles of the lunar surface, testing all of its systems. After returning to the command module and joining Young inside, they ditched the LEM and headed back to Earth. The mission was a complete success. Everything was now in place for Apollo 11 and a landing on the moon.

In their roles as head of the astronaut office and director of flight crew operations, Alan and Deke had established a system for choosing the astronauts for each Apollo mission. To every mission was assigned a primary crew as well as a complete backup crew. If the backup crew was not used, it would become the primary crew for the mission three flights later. The next flight, Apollo 11, belonged to Neil Armstrong, Mike Collins, and Buzz Aldrin. Alan knew that there was no way he could elbow his way onto the schedule for that flight. Instead he chose to maneuver his way onto the backup crew for Apollo 10, which was now the primary crew for Apollo 13. He was successful in his effort, and Deke replaced Gordon Cooper with Alan as commander of Apollo 13. Of course Cooper was not at all happy with the situation. But despite his protests about the change, it soon became obvious that within NASA there was a lot of support to send America's first man in space to the moon.

When NASA managers in Washington, D.C., heard of the decision to put Alan on Apollo 13, they were not sure that he could be thoroughly trained for the flight in the available timeframe before the mission was scheduled to blast off. They insisted that Alan wait one more flight before heading to the moon. The crew of Apollo 14 was moved forward to fly Apollo 13, while Alan and his crew were moved to Apollo 14.

Alan began a rigorous training schedule to prepare himself for the mission. Astronauts on the Apollo project were expected to be more than just pilots. They had to be experts in a range of subjects, everything from computers to rocket propulsion, physics, meteorology, and geology, the latter subjects being important when they got to the surface of the moon and had to carry out complex experiments as well as collect rock and soil samples. The astronauts also had to be able to fly both the Apollo command module and the lunar excursion module. They had to know how to navigate by the stars, so that if something went wrong with their navigation system during the mission, they could find their way back to Earth. This was a far cry from Project Mercury, where Alan just had to fly the spacecraft. Soon Alan was spending hours in the classroom learning from some of the world's most knowledgeable people. He also spent hours on end in flight simulators, learning how to fly the command module and the LEM.

Meanwhile, all eyes were on the Apollo 11 flight to the moon. No one was sure how the mission would go. Even if the LEM did land safely on the moon, what would it be landing on? Some scientists speculated that the moon's surface might be like quicksand and swallow up the craft, while others thought that it could be sticky and that nothing that landed on it could take off again. No one knew for sure. They would all just have to wait and see and hope for the best.

On July 16, 1969, Alan took time out from his rigorous training schedule and traveled to Kennedy Space Center with Louise and their three daughters to view the liftoff of Apollo 11.

Alan was standing in the VIP viewing section staring at the massive Saturn V rocket sitting in the launchpad three miles away and thinking about his upcoming launch atop the powerful behemoth, when an old man in a crumpled suit and hat approached him. Alan recognized the man immediately. "Captain Shepard," the man said, stretching out his hand to shake Alan's, "I'm Charles Lindbergh."

Alan shook Lindbergh's hand warmly and then introduced the aviator to Louise and his daughters.

As the countdown for Apollo 11 continued, the two men took a stroll together. Alan told Lindbergh how his 1927 flight across the Atlantic had inspired him as a boy to want to fly, and Lindbergh told Alan how heroic and inspiring his flight on *Freedom 7* had been. As they talked, they realized that there were a lot of similarities between their two historic flights. Both flights had been dangerous and uncertain, both became intertwined with politics, and the two of them had had to deal with the ever-present crush of reporters and photographers.

The two aviation pioneers talked together for half an hour and then stood shoulder to shoulder as the Saturn V rocket burst to life and lifted Apollo 11 into space in a breathtaking blaze of orange flame.

The flight of Apollo 11 to the moon was flawless, and three days after liftoff, Alan stood in a control room at Kennedy Space Center and watched and listened as Neil Armstrong guided the LEM, which was named *Eagle*, down to the surface of the moon. There were a couple of glitches along the way. A warning flashed that the onboard computer was overloaded, but NASA's computer whiz, Steven Bales, told them it would be fine to continue with the descent; and Armstrong had been forced to make some last-minute maneuvers when it was discovered that the chosen landing site was covered in boulders. They were anxious moments for all at NASA, but *Eagle* eventually settled gently onto the moon's surface in an area known as the Sea of Tranquility. A cheer went up when the radio crackled with Armstrong's announcement, "The *Eagle* has landed." The United States had won the space race, at least this leg of it. It had landed not one, but two men on the moon!

An even bigger cheer went up when six and a half hours later Armstrong began his descent down the ladder from the lunar excursion module to the surface of the moon. As he stepped onto the lunar surface, he declared, "That's one small step for man, one giant leap for mankind."

Fifteen minutes later, Buzz Aldrin joined Neil Armstrong on the surface of the moon, where he declared of the lunar landscape, "Beautiful. Beautiful. Magnificent desolation."

The two astronauts spent two and a half hours walking on the surface of the moon and collecting

rock samples to take back to Earth. Then they
climbed back into the LEM for a rest period. Twenty-
one and a half hours after landing on the moon,
Eagle blasted off to return the two astronauts to
the command module orbiting above and being
piloted by Michael Collins.

On July 24, the Apollo 11 capsule splashed
down in the North Pacific Ocean, its mission a complete and resounding success. While Alan would
have liked nothing better than to have been on
Apollo 11 himself, his chest puffed with pride at
NASA's and America's achievement.

Upon their return home, the three Apollo 11
astronauts were welcomed as heroes. They were
easily the most famous men in the world. Even
kindergarten children could recite their names and
how long they had stood on the moon.

Two weeks after the return of Apollo 11, NASA
officially announced to the public that America's
first man in space, Alan Shepard, was going back
to space as commander of Apollo 14. With him on
the flight would be Stuart Roosa, who would serve
as the command-module pilot, and Edgar Mitchell,
the lunar-excursion-module pilot who would
accompany Alan down to the surface of the moon.

On November 12, 1969, Apollo 12 blasted off
from Kennedy Space Center and successfully delivered two more Americans, Pete Conrad and Alan
Bean, to the surface of the moon and their place in
the history books. Next came Apollo 13, the flight
Alan had been "bumped" from to Apollo 14. Like
the previous two flights to the moon, Apollo 13 was

expected to be another near-perfect mission to explore the lowlands of the moon.

After blasting off from Kennedy Space Center, Apollo 13 headed for the moon. On April 13, 1970, two days after liftoff and two hundred thousand miles from Earth, something went terribly wrong with the mission. A violent explosion reverberated through the spacecraft. Immediately astronaut Jack Swigert radioed mission control in Houston declaring, "Okay, Houston, we've had a problem here." Moments later mission commander Jim Lovell was also on the radio. "Ah, Houston, we have a problem."

It turned out to be a big problem. One of the oxygen tanks located in the service module attached beneath the Apollo capsule had exploded, tearing a hole in the side of the service module. To make matters worse, the explosion had damaged the second oxygen tank, which was now venting its precious supply of oxygen into space. This oxygen not only provided air for the astronauts but also powered the fuel cell that produced electricity for the spacecraft. Quickly the three astronauts powered down the command module to conserve what little electricity they had left. With no oxygen supply in the command module, the three men scrambled into the lunar excursion module to use this vehicle's oxygen supply.

On the ground in Houston, astronauts, engineers, and mission controllers sprang into action. They had never before encountered a situation like this, and they scrambled to find a way to get the crew of Apollo 13 back home safely. Alan quickly assigned astronauts to flight simulators to come up with a way to fly the damaged spacecraft. He was relentless and tireless in his efforts. He realized that if things had not played out the way they had, he could have easily been aboard Apollo 13, and he knew that if he were, he would want people on the ground to do everything possible to try to get him safely back home.

Meanwhile, using things available in the space-craft, engineers came up with an ingenious way to make a scrubber that could filter the carbon dioxide from the air inside the LEM. After many simulations it was decided that the best way to get the astronauts back to Earth was to let the damaged craft coast to the moon and then use the moon's gravity to slingshot it back toward Earth.

Alan waited anxiously as Apollo 13 carried on toward the moon and then was slung back toward Earth. He knew how uncomfortable it must be for the three astronauts aboard. The men were crammed at near-freezing temperatures into a spacecraft designed to hold only two, and they were breathing a supply of oxygen meant to keep two men alive for two days. Not only that, but the three of them were trying to make this oxygen supply stretch out for the four days it would take them to get back to Earth. Alan could only guess at the fear and apprehension they must have been feeling.

Somehow the Apollo 13 astronauts were able to hang on. As their spacecraft approached Earth, they were able to power up the command module, separate from the LEM and the damaged service module, and reenter Earth's atmosphere. They splashed down in the Pacific Ocean just two and a half miles from the recovery ship USS *Iwo Jima*, making it the most accurate landing of all the Apollo missions.

Alan breathed a sigh of relief when he heard that Jim Lovell, Jack Swigert, and Fred Haise were safely aboard the *Iwo Jima*. He also wondered how the events of Apollo 13 would affect his upcoming flight.

In light of the near disaster of Apollo 13, NASA officials decided to delay the launch of Apollo 14 for four months while they investigated. The cause of the explosion was eventually tracked down to a damaged wire. Modifications were made to the service module on Apollo 14 to prevent such a situation from happening again. A third oxygen tank was fitted to the module, this one isolated in such a way that it would not be damaged by an explosion. Another battery was also added, ensuring that if another emergency occurred, there would be enough power to get the astronauts home. The new launch date for the mission was set for January 14, 1971—nine years and eight months after Alan had blasted into space aboard *Freedom 7*.

As the launch date drew nearer, Alan felt like a child waiting for Christmas. At the same time he noticed that Louise was becoming more and more nervous. Alan tried to assure her that everything with the mission would be fine, but with the failure

of Apollo 13 mission fresh in everyone's mind, it
was a hard sell. Alan remained confident, however.
He was going to the moon!

Chapter 17

Fra Mauro Base

It was early afternoon, Thursday, January 31, 1971, and Alan Shepard stood in his bulky space suit and stared up at the huge Saturn V rocket that towered above him. It was quite a sight. The rocket creaked as the frigid liquid oxygen and hydrogen was pressurized in the vehicle's fuel tanks. Already the sides of the rocket were covered in ice from the rocket's freezing contents. Alan thought back almost ten years to another launchpad located across the Banana River from where he stood. That morning as he prepared to fly on *Freedom 7,* he had also stopped and looked up at the rocket. The sight of the Redstone had awed him. Then, he had been on his way to a fifteen-minute flight into space; today he was going to traverse a quarter of a million miles of space to stand on the moon. And like ten

years before, words failed Alan as he contemplated
what lay ahead.

Alan, Stuart Roosa, and Edgar Mitchell stepped
into the elevator and rode up the four hundred feet
to the Apollo capsule. The massive Saturn V rocket
was nearly five times as tall as the Redstone had
been. At the top, workers helped the men slide into
the capsule, which they had named *Kitty Hawk,*
and made sure that they were strapped in and their
space suits were properly connected to the life-
support system. When everything was taken care
of, the workers wished the three astronauts good
luck and closed the hatch with a thud.

The countdown began, and Alan felt the same
butterflies as he had when he waited for *Freedom 7*
to launch. As he had done then, he concentrated on
the preflight check of the capsule's instruments.

The countdown reached ten minutes to go, and
everything was progressing perfectly on schedule.
But when they reached eight minutes to go, the
countdown was put on hold. Ground controllers
radioed to say that a storm front had blown in and
they were going to wait for it to pass over Kennedy
Space Center and head out to sea. Alan felt frustration rising within him. He was ready to fly, and that
is what he wanted to do. He didn't want to be stuck
on the launchpad for hours as he had been on
Freedom 7. But he could do nothing about the situation as heavy rain pelted against the Apollo capsule and the Saturn V rocket.

Finally, after a wait of forty minutes, the storm
front passed and the countdown resumed. Soon

they were into the last ten seconds of the count-down. At nine seconds to go, Alan heard the ground controller say, "Ignition sequence start." That signaled the start of the Saturn V's five huge main engines. Alan knew that below them, thousands of gallons of fuel were now being pumped into the engines, which ignited the rocket and belched out in a fireball of thrust, though high up in *Kitty Hawk* he could hear none of the thunderous noise the rocket produced.

"Five...Four...Three...Two...One...All engines running...Zero..." came the voice of the controller over the radio.

When the clock hit zero, the arms that held the rocket in place while its engines came up to full power sprang back and released the mighty Saturn V, which immediately began to rise, a blizzard of ice showering from its sides as it rose. It was 4:03 PM, and Apollo 14 was on its way.

Inside *Kitty Hawk* Alan was surprised at how smooth and quiet their ascent into space was. He was aware of a gentle rumble far below, but there was none of the noise and vibration that he had experienced on *Freedom 7*. And after they climbed through the speed of sound, even the rumbling sound faded away, and an eerie silence filled the capsule.

Two and a half minutes into the flight, the force of gravity on his body made Alan feel four times heavier than normal. They were now forty miles high and traveling at six thousand miles per hour. Alan braced himself and waited for the jolt that was about to come as the first stage of the rocket, its fuel spent, detached and the second-stage engines kicked in. Soon after the second stage of the rocket kicked in, the escape tower on the nose of *Kitty Hawk* blasted away, no longer needed.

Eleven minutes after liftoff, and one hundred fifty miles up, the second stage dropped away and the engine of the third stage kicked in. Two minutes later the third-stage engine cut out. *Kitty Hawk* was now in Earth orbit traveling at 17,400 miles per hour.

Alan released the harness that held him in his seat and immediately floated up in the weightlessness of space. To Alan, who had remained strapped into his seat during his *Freedom 7* flight, the feeling of floating freely was exhilarating. He told himself that the feeling was almost worth the entire trip.

After two and a half hours in Earth orbit, Mission Control in Houston radioed to say that everything checked out with the spacecraft. The controller then said, "Apollo 14, you are Go for translunar injection."

Alan was elated when he heard these words. It was time to head for the moon.

Moments later the third-stage engine reignited, hurling Alan back against his seat as it blasted the men out of orbit and put them on a course for the moon. By the time the engine cut out, they were traveling at 24,500 miles per hour, though inside *Kitty Hawk* it seemed as if they were hardly moving.

It was not long after the third-stage engine cut out that Alan's feeling of elation turned to frustration and dread—frustration that something seemed to be wrong with the docking clamps on the space-craft, and dread that this problem might mean they could not land on the moon.

Stuart Roosa, the command-module pilot, had separated Apollo 14 from the third-stage rocket, turned the craft around, and docked with the lunar excursion module housed on top of the spent third-stage rocket. But for some reason the clamps that were supposed to lock the two vehicles together would not activate. Stuart backed the command module off and tried the maneuver again, and still the clamps would not operate. He tried the maneu-ver a third time, with the same result.

Engineers on the ground in Houston tried to troubleshoot the problem. Over the next hour the astronauts made three more attempts to dock with the LEM, and each time the clamps failed to engage. Things were getting desperate. The repeated maneuver was eating away at the precious fuel supply. Finally it was decided to make one last attempt to dock. If the clamps did not engage this time, the lunar-landing mission would have to be aborted, and Apollo 14 would then undertake a secondary mission, abandoning the LEM and trav-eling on to the moon, where they would orbit and photograph the lunar surface using the new high-definition camera installed on the spacecraft. But that is not what Alan wanted. He wanted to go down to the surface of the moon.

On the final docking attempt, engineers on the ground told the astronauts to fire the capsule's rockets and try a hard docking with the LEM. Perhaps this might shake the clamps free, they reasoned.

Stuart backed off one last time and lined *Kitty Hawk* up with the LEM, and then Alan told him to gun the rockets. *Kitty Hawk* and the LEM came together with a thump. But still the men did not hear the metallic ringing of the clamps activating. Alan's heart sank. He would not be walking on the moon, after all. But as he began to descend into a pit of despair, a green light on the instrument panel flashed on, and the men heard the sound of the clamps activating. "Houston, we've got a hard dock," Stuart radioed as Alan felt his spirits soar.

Stuart backed *Kitty Hawk* off, this time with the LEM, which Edgar Mitchell had named *Antares,* in tow. After pulling the LEM free of the third-stage rocket, the men were on their way to the moon.

On the way to the moon Alan had difficulty sleeping. He was much too excited to sleep as adrenaline coursed through his body. But while he may have had trouble sleeping, he did not have trouble eating. He was constantly popping open cans and devouring their contents and squeezing tubes of various food substances into his mouth.

Much to Alan's relief, Apollo 14 eventually settled into orbit around the moon. Now it was time for Alan and Edgar Mitchell to don their bulky space suits and crawl into *Antares* for the descent to the lunar surface.

While Stuart piloted *Kitty Hawk,* Alan and Edgar undocked *Antares* and began their descent.

But they soon ran into problems. A signal light on
the LEM's instrument panel lit up, signaling that
the vehicle's abort program had been triggered.
Alan and Edgar looked at each other with a look
that said, "Surely it's a malfunction?" Edgar tapped
the control panel with a gloved finger, and the light
went out. Alan breathed a sigh of relief, but a few
minutes later the warning light blinked on again.
Once more Edgar tapped the control panel with his
finger and the light went out. Alan and Edgar
decided that the problem was a loose piece of solder
in the control panel which, as it floated around in
the weightlessness of space, triggered the abort
sequence warning light. But this presented them
with a problem. Once the LEM began to close in on
the lunar surface, if the abort warning went off, the
vehicle's onboard computer was programmed to
automatically fire *Antares*'s rockets and blast the
craft back into orbit. If that happened during their
final descent, they could be blasted back too far
into space and not be able to rejoin *Kitty Hawk*.
They had a ninety-minute window of opportunity to
make their descent to the moon or they would have
to abort the mission.

Alan talked over the situation with ground controllers in Houston, who told him they were working on a fix to the problem. Alan waited anxiously
to see what they would come up with. He would
later learn that back on Earth, Donald Eyles, an
engineer at MIT, was awakened at two in the morning in Massachusetts by an air force officer pound-
ing on his apartment door. The officer explained the

situation, and Eyles, still dressed in his pajamas, raced to his computer lab at MIT.

Donald Eyles was the engineer who had written the code that ran *Antares*'s onboard computer. He quickly set to work writing a new piece of code that would tell the computer to ignore and override the faulty abort warning. It took him an hour to complete the job. The new code was immediately radioed to Mission Control in Houston, where mission controllers loaded the code into the computer of a flight simulator and tested it. The new code worked and was radioed up to the LEM. Using the small keyboard on the control panel, Edgar Mitchell then proceeded to painstakingly key the code into *Antares*'s computer. It was a difficult job, especially since his fingers were encased in a bulky space suit. The descent window was closing fast, and Alan grew anxious, willing Edgar to go faster, though he knew he couldn't. One wrong keystroke while entering the code could spell disaster for them. It took about five minutes to key in the code, leaving them with only fifteen minutes to descend to the moon.

Alan swung into action, firing *Antares*'s retro-rockets, slowing the LEM, and guiding it down toward the moon. But because of the LEM's angle as it approached the moon, the vehicle's windows were facing up toward space, and Alan had to rely on his instruments and radar to guide him down. That was when the second problem occurred. Suddenly the radar screen in *Antares* lost its lock on the lunar surface. Alan could scarcely believe it.

He continued his descent, flying blind, but NASA rules forbade him from descending below ten thousand feet without a radar lock, and that altitude was fast approaching. A controller in Houston radioed to remind them of the rule.

"We're aware of the rule, Houston," a frustrated Alan radioed back.

Aware of the rule or not, Alan was less than three miles above the surface of the moon, and he was not about to give up now. He was prepared to fly *Antares* the entire way down blind if need be. After all, no one from NASA was around to enforce the rule. Alan told Edgar of his scheme, and Edgar concurred. They had come too far to give up now.

As they were contemplating breaking the rule, Mission Control radioed with what could be a simple fix to the problem. Alan did as they told him, reaching over and pulling out the circuit breaker for the radar system and then reinserting it. But still there was no radar lock. And then almost magically, at fourteen thousand feet above the moon, the radar suddenly started working normally again, locking in on the lunar surface and displaying crisp, clear images on the screen in front of Alan. Alan gave a thumbs-up, radioed the good news to Mission Control, and continued with the descent.

Antares was descending into a region known as Fra Mauro, where the crew of Apollo 13 had been scheduled to land and explore. This was a rocky, hilly region of the moon that scientists believed contained some of the universe's oldest rocks. In particular, NASA scientists had chosen for the LEM a landing site located close to a depression in the lunar surface they called Cone Crater. As Alan descended toward the landing spot, he could see that Fra Mauro was a wild and desolate place. As he got closer to the surface, he began having to make some quick maneuvers to dodge ridges and bumps as the LEM moved toward a flat, clear patch of land, where he finally guided *Antares* down to a landing. He had landed within fifty feet of the spot chosen by the scientists, closer to the target than the two previous lunar landings. "Right on the money," he radioed back to mission control.

Antares was safely down. Alan Shepard had arrived on the moon!

Alan dropped the three and a half feet from the bottom rung of the nine-rung ladder onto the surface of the moon. A cloud of talc-like lunar dust puffed up as his feet touched down. He looked around at the barren landscape they had landed in. Large boulders were strewn around, and the surface was covered with pockmarks. Unlike the previous two lunar missions, which had landed on broad, open mares, or seas, *Antares* had landed in a low, rock-strewn valley, a place of utter desolation baked by a blazing sun and completely silent. Strong emotions surged through Alan as he scanned the landscape. Then he looked up into the black sky and there saw a sight he would never forget. The earth, a blue-green sphere dusted with white, hung above the moon's horizon. It had seemed so big and permanent when they blasted off three days before. But slowly, as they traversed toward the moon, it had receded in scale, and now it looked like a precarious ball in the distance. Yet the sight of it was awe-inspiring—that fragile ball above the horizon was home, and Alan Shepard was seeing Earth in a way only four people before him had ever seen it—from the surface of the moon.

Alan brought his mind back to his present situation. "Al is on the surface. It's been a long way, but we're here," he radioed to mission control.

"Not bad for an old man," came the reply from Houston.

Inside his space suit Alan smiled. Indeed, it had been a long journey for him to get to this point. But he had persevered, and now he had arrived. At forty-seven years of age, he was the oldest man to stand on the moon.

Three minutes after stepping onto the lunar surface, Alan watched as Edgar made his way down the ladder to join him. After Edgar had taken a few moments to take in the sights around him, the two men got to work. The first thing they did was set up a tripod with a remote television camera atop it sixty feet from *Antares* so that people on Earth could see both the LEM and the two of them at work around it. On this mission they were using a new color television camera. Once the camera was up and running, they placed an American flag in the ground.

Stowed beneath *Antares* was a new contraption called a modularized equipment transporter, or MET, a wheelbarrow-like device for transporting science equipment and rock and soil samples. Once they had unloaded the MET, or "lunar rickshaw," as the astronauts preferred to call it, they began setting up the equipment for various science experiments. Once the experiments were under way, they took the lunar rickshaw and, using the array of tools loaded in it, began to scoop up soil samples and various rocks. They brought the samples and rocks back to *Antares*, sealed them in vacuum bags, and hoisted them up into the upper stage of the spacecraft to be returned with them to Earth.

Alan had to admit that even in the moon's one-sixth gravity, it was hard work. And while the ground where the previous two lunar missions had landed was fairly firm under foot, the surface of Fra Mauro was loose and mushy and made it hard to maneuver the lunar rickshaw. It felt more often like they were dragging it through sand than wheeling it along. And walking was proving to be an interesting challenge. The low gravity made it feel to Alan like he was walking on a trampoline on Earth. To move around, Alan found that he needed to lean forward and take more of a skipping step than a walking step. Still, despite the hard work, it was exhilarating to be doing it on the moon.

After the men had spent five hours on the lunar surface, Mission Control radioed that it was time for them to rest. Alan and Edgar dusted the powdery lunar soil off their boots and space suits as best they could and ascended the ladder back into *Antares*. They ate and drank and then pulled themselves into their hammocks to sleep. Neither man got much sleep. The LEM had not been built for comfort. The air-conditioning unit inside the craft hissed and moaned, and the thin aluminum walls seemed to emit strange noises. To make matters worse, Edgar kept sliding up the shades over the windows for a look outside, flooding the compartment with bright sunlight.

The two astronauts were supposed to take a ten-hour rest break, but after only eight hours they radioed Houston that they were up and ready to go. They climbed back down onto the lunar surface and began their next day's activities, a trek to the rim of Cone Crater to photograph and explore it and bring back more rock samples. They estimated that the crater rim was about a mile away, and they set out with the lunar rickshaw in tow. However, the going was slow, and eventually they decided to leave the rickshaw behind because it was proving too difficult to maneuver, and they were expending too much energy trying to pull it along.

Even without the lunar rickshaw in tow, the mission proved difficult. The harsh sun burned the exposed landscape to a bright white and cast long shadows that created strange optical illusions, which made it hard sometimes to tell where they were. Still as best they could, Alan and Edgar tried to keep moving forward. The up-and-down terrain and the large boulders they had to make their way around also made the job difficult. Alan was sweating and gasping for oxygen inside his space suit. Eventually Mission Control in Houston advised the men to cancel their goal of reaching the crater's edge and to instead concentrate on collecting more rock and soil samples. And that is what the two astronauts did, eventually making it back to *Antares* after their lunar trek.

Once the rock and soil samples were safely stowed aboard the LEM, it was time for Alan and Edgar to climb back aboard the *Antares* and rejoin Stuart Roosa orbiting above in *Kitty Hawk*. But before they left the moon, Alan had a little surprise for the controllers back in Houston. From one of his space-suit pockets he pulled the head of a golf club, a six iron. He attached the head to one of the poles he had used for collecting samples to form an improvised golf club. Then he reached into his pocket and pulled out a ball. "In my left hand I have a little white pellet that's familiar to millions of Americans," he announced to mission control.

Alan dropped the ball onto the lunar surface and then lined himself up as best he could in his bulky space suit and took a swing at the ball with his improvised club. There was a spray of dust, and the ball moved about a hundred feet. "I got more dirt than ball," Alan said, and with that he pulled another golf ball from his pocket and dropped it. Once again he lined himself up and swung his club. This time he did much better, hitting the ball squarely and sending it careening off across the landscape in the low lunar gravity. "Beautiful! There it goes! Miles and miles and miles!"

Alan Shepard was the first astronaut—first man—to play golf on the moon!

Once he had made his golf shots, Alan checked the area around the *Antares* to make sure that everything to be returned to Earth was loaded aboard the module. Then he walked over, looked into the television camera, and declared, "Houston, the crew of *Antares* is leaving Fra Mauro Base." With that, he followed Edgar up the ladder into the LEM. His time on the moon was over. Alan took one last look at the landscape he had called home for the past thirty-three hours, and then he closed the hatch.

After blasting off from the moon, *Antares* docked with *Kitty Hawk.* While Alan and Edgar had been on the moon, Stuart had orbited above, taking detailed photographs of the lunar surface.

Once Alan and Edgar had transferred all of the samples they had collected from the LEM to the command module, they closed and sealed the hatch between the two vehicles and then Stuart released the LEM. Its mission complete, the LEM was no longer needed and was left behind to eventually crash onto the moon. As he backed *Kitty Hawk* away from the LEM, Stuart said, "And we say sayonara, good-bye, to *Antares.*" Alan felt a tinge of sadness as he watched the craft drift away.

Soon after *Antares* had drifted free, Mission Control gave the okay to head for Earth. Stuart fired the command module's engine to break out of orbit and set them on course for home, and they were on their way. Three days later *Kitty Hawk* floated to a perfect splashdown in the Pacific Ocean, where the aircraft carrier USS *New Orleans* was waiting nearby to pick them up. Alan was back on Earth, but in the past nine days he had been higher and gone faster than most men had ever dreamed was possible, and more important, he had made it back into space.

Chapter 18

A True American Hero

We need to put you on a diet!" the nurse joked as she weighed Alan in the quarantine room, where the three Apollo 14 astronauts had been taken after being recovered from their capsule in the Pacific Ocean. "You've put on a pound in nine days. Every other astronaut has lost weight in space. Jim Lovell lost fourteen pounds during Apollo 13."

Alan chuckled to himself. He had always had a hearty appetite, and being in space hadn't changed that. Then he tucked into a large tray of bacon, eggs, and toast, his first meal after arriving back on Earth.

When the quarantine period was over, Alan, Stuart, and Edgar emerged to a raucous welcome. Thousands of men, women, and children showed up at the various ceremonies, galas, and parades to honor the success of the Apollo 14 mission. Millions more people saw the three astronauts on television as they made the customary visit to the White House and a meeting with President Richard Nixon. The president awarded Alan the title of "first celestial hole in one" for his golf swing on the moon.

A month later another honor followed for Alan Shepard when the navy promoted him to the rank of rear admiral. Alan was the only astronaut to attain the rank and one of only a few navy admirals never to have commanded a ship. Many years before, Alan had chosen to become an astronaut over the promotional path he was on in the navy that he had hoped would lead to the rank of admiral. Now he was both. He couldn't wait to show his father his new insignia, and soon afterward he had the opportunity to visit his elderly parents in New Hampshire.

After dinner with his parents and Louise, Alan sat in the living room with his father the "colonel," chatting. His father was the first to broach the subject.

"Do you remember when you first told us back in 1959 that you were going to become an astronaut?"

"Yes, sir," Alan replied.

"Do you remember what I said?"

Alan remembered what his father had said as if it were yesterday: his father had made him feel like a traitor to the family name. Alan nodded. "You were not in favor of it."

Bart Shepard lifted his glass in a toast to his son. "Well, I was wrong."

Alan smiled. He knew how hard that was for his father to admit, and he was deeply satisfied that his father finally appreciated the contribution Alan had made to science and America's faith in itself.

With the Apollo 14 mission behind him, things began to wind down for Alan at NASA, and he knew that he would soon retire. In the meantime, he was "loaned" out for various matters of public interest and service. George H. W. Bush, U.S. ambassador to the United Nations, requested that Alan serve as a delegate to the 26th United Nations General Assembly. President Nixon appointed Alan to the position in July 1971, and Alan served as a delegate throughout the entire assembly, which lasted from September to December 1971.

Although being chosen to serve as a delegate to the United Nations was a great honor, the experience proved to Alan that his heart was not really in politics. He had spent the twelve years since becoming an astronaut trying to avoid the press and personal attention, and becoming a politician like fellow Mercury Seven astronaut John Glenn would only invite one hundred times more press scrutiny. Instead Alan continued to serve in his role as chief of the astronaut office at the Manned Spacecraft Center in Houston. (The name of the center was changed to the Johnson Space Center in 1973 in honor of President Lyndon Johnson.) Finally, on August 1, 1974, Alan Shepard officially retired from NASA and the navy.

With his NASA and navy careers over, Alan turned to business to occupy his time. He had always made successful investments, and now with more time on his hands, he dived deeper into investing. He sold the bank shares he had for over six thousand dollars and invested the money in another growing company. He also invested in a Detroit-based company called Kresge, which owned a fast-growing chain of discount department stores and would soon change its name to Kmart Corporation. Both of these investments went very well, making Alan a multimillionaire.

After leaving NASA, Alan continued to maintain a low public profile, keeping his wife and growing family of sons-in-law and grandchildren out of the limelight. He and Louise had many famous, rich friends, but for the most part, Alan lost touch with his astronaut buddies, that is, until 1979 when a book called *The Right Stuff* exploded onto the best-seller list. The book's author, Tom Wolfe, had written a compelling tale of the Mercury Seven, bringing back memories of heroism and drama that had been overlooked by the new generation. Suddenly Alan and the other Mercury Seven astronauts were again heroes!

The book was turned into a movie in 1983, and the American public began clamoring to see the remaining six members of the Mercury Seven together again in one place. Invitations for personal appearances flowed in, and grudgingly at first Alan was drawn back into the astronaut circle. He later accepted that his achievements in space were going to define the rest of his life.

About this time an old friend, an innkeeper near Cape Canaveral named Henri Landwirth, came up with an idea. Why not use this new exposure for good? he reasoned. Why couldn't the Mercury Seven, actually six of them and Gus Grissom's widow, Betty, start a charity to raise scholarship money for needy children interested in math and science careers? And so the Mercury Seven Foundation was born. Alan and the others got behind the new foundation, which slowly began to make enough money to provide modest scholarships.

Alan gave all of the money he received from personal appearances to the foundation, and at the same time he used his renown to raise money for a deaf school in Houston.

In 1989 Alan and Louise decided it was time for a change, and they moved from Houston to Pebble Beach, California. They had always enjoyed the California coastline, and now they bought a beautiful home overlooking the craggy rocks and swelling surf of the Pacific Ocean.

By 1990 the Mercury Seven Foundation was renamed the Astronaut Scholarship Foundation, and it continued to blossom. Already it had given out a million dollars in scholarships, and it had plans to expand even more. A second charity, the Space Camp Foundation, grew out of it, and the Astronaut Scholarship Foundation also helped to fund the Astronaut Hall of Fame and gift shop, located near the Kennedy Space Center in Florida.

Alan spent many weeks each year drumming up money for these causes, along with one other. Henri Landwirth started another charity called Give Kids the World. He had transformed fifty acres of land in Central Florida into a huge hotel/adventureland where terminally ill children and their families could come to enjoy happy times together. Henri asked Alan to do what he could to help with the project, and in turn Alan persuaded Kmart into becoming a major sponsor of the facility.

Another project also took up a significant portion of Alan's time. In 1992 Deke Slayton had begun work on a book about the race to the moon from the astronauts' perspective. Deke enlisted Neil Armstrong to help him with the project, and Alan had no desire to be a part of it. He liked the press to know as little about him as possible.

During the writing of the book, however, Deke was diagnosed with a brain tumor, and Neil pulled out of the project. Alan wanted to do whatever he could to raise his old friend's spirits, so he agreed to help Deke finish the book. They had just put the finishing touches on the manuscript in 1993 when Deke died. Once the book, called *Moon Shot,* was published, Alan threw his efforts into promoting it in the hope that money from its sale could provide an ongoing income for Deke's widow.

Now there were five members of the Mercury Seven remaining, and secretly Alan wondered who would be the next to go. Though he was now seventy years old, he was enjoying good health, skiing regularly, playing golf, and having regular medical checkups, so he was fairly confident that he would not be the next to die. Then in 1996 a new word invaded Alan's life—leukemia, cancer of the blood

and bone marrow that leads to an abnormal prolif-
eration of white blood cells.

Alan had begun to feel weak and tired, and for
the first time in his life his appetite was poor and
he was losing weight. He sought medical advice, and
after running several tests, his doctor made the
diagnosis. Alan had leukemia, and according to the
doctor, little could be done for him. Alan told only
Louise and the children about the diagnosis and
determined to find a way to go on as best he could.

Because he was seventy-three when he was
diagnosed with leukemia, Alan was not eligible for a
bone-marrow transplant, the only treatment that
doctors said could prolong his life significantly.
Instead he was treated with blood transfusions,
during which most of his old, white-cell-laden blood
was drained from his body and replaced by fresh
blood rich in red cells and platelets.

Alan read up on all he could about leukemia
and consulted every medical specialist he thought
might be able to help him with his disease, but by
1997 he was ready to face the fact that he was
dying. He was not, however, ready to stop living the
best life he could.

In late 1997 Alan and Louise traveled to Orlando,
Florida, to attend the annual Astronaut Scholarship
Foundation meeting and dinner. It was a particularly poignant time as Alan stepped down as head
of the foundation and fellow astronaut Jim Lovell
took his place.

At the end of the evening, Don Engen, a former
navy pilot and head of the National Air and Space

Museum, stepped to the podium. He had a broad smile on his face as he spoke. "You've been bugging me about this for years, Al," he said. "Well, I give up. Apollo 14 is all yours."

Alan felt Louise squeeze his hand; she too knew what Don meant. The Apollo 14 capsule had been put on display at the Smithsonian National Air and Space Museum in Washington, D.C., following the mission, and Alan had wanted it to be donated to the Astronaut Hall of Fame so that it would draw larger crowds to the facility, thus creating more revenue for the Astronaut Scholarship Foundation. Alan waved at the exciting news, but he didn't trust himself to speak.

The following day Alan traveled to the Astronaut Hall of Fame, where a ceremony was held to unveil the Apollo 14 capsule *Kitty Hawk* in its new home. The other members of the Mercury Seven stood by as Alan walked slowly up to the capsule that had supported him for nine days as he hurtled half a million miles through space, all the way to the moon and back. As Alan reached out and touched *Kitty Hawk*, suddenly the years rolled back. For once, Alan Shepard could not help himself. He began to weep, quietly at first and then more loudly, until his entire frail body shook.

That was to be Alan's last major public appearance. Alan lived quietly at home after that, traveling regularly to the hospital in nearby Monterey, California, for treatments, talking on the phone to his daughters, and sipping coffee with Louise on the back porch overlooking the ocean.

Late on Tuesday night, July 21, 1998, Alan Shepard died in his sleep. He was seventy-four years old.

The next day headlines around the world proclaimed the death of "One Cool Moonwalker" and "America's Lindbergh of Space." George W. S. Abbey, Director of the Johnson Space Center in Houston, wrote in his eulogy,

> Alan Shepard is a true American hero, a pioneer, an original. He was part of a courageous corps of astronauts that allowed us to reach out into space and venture into the unknown. Alan Shepard gave all of us the privilege to participate in the beginnings of America's great adventure of human space exploration. He will be greatly missed. The program has lost one of its greatest supporters and a true friend.... Alan Shepard lived to explore the heavens. On this final journey, we wish him Godspeed.

NASA also held a memorial service at the Johnson Space Center. The four remaining Mercury Seven astronauts were in attendance, and each one tried to speak, though Wally Schirra left the podium sobbing, and the other three did not fare much better. A tree was planted on the grounds of the space center in memory of Alan, and four navy jets roared overhead, one peeling off midway through in the missing-man formation that signified a pilot down. Tears streamed down people's cheeks as the crowd watched this final tribute to an incredibly brave pilot who had fought for his chance to go all the way to the moon and back.

Following Alan's death, family members wondered how Louise would go on without him, and she didn't for long. After the death of her husband, Louise went to stay with her daughter Laura. Five weeks later she felt strong enough to return home to face their empty house at Pebble Beach. She was onboard a small plane flying from San Francisco to Monterey when her heart stopped beating. There was nothing anyone could do to save her.

Ironically, Louise Shepard died in an airplane flying over the Pacific Ocean, while her risk-defying, jet-pilot husband had died on land.

Louise's body was cremated, as had Alan's been, and close friends and family gathered to watch their ashes mingle as they drifted down into the cold water of the Pacific Ocean that surged in the rocky inlet behind their home at Pebble Beach.

Glenn, John. *John Glenn: A Memoir.* Bantam Books, 1999.

Mackinnon, Douglas, and Joseph Baldanza. *Footprints: The 12 Men Who Walked on the Moon Reflect on Their Flights, Their Lives, and the Future.* Acropolis Books, 1989.

Reynolds, David West. *Apollo: The Epic Journey to the Moon.* Harcourt, 2002.

Shepard, Alan, and Deke Slayton. *Moon Shot: The Inside Story of America's Race to the Moon.* Turner Publishing, 1994.

Thompson, Neal. *Light This Candle: The Life and Times of Alan Shepard.* Three Rivers Press, 2004.

Janet and Geoff Benge are a husband and wife writing team with more than twenty years of writing experience. Janet is a former elementary-school teacher. Geoff holds a degree in history. Together they have a passion to make history come alive for a new generation of readers.

Originally from New Zealand, the Benges make their home in the Orlando, Florida, area.

Also from Janet and Geoff Benge...

More adventure-filled biographies for ages 10 to 100!

Also available:

Unit Study Curriculum Guides

Turn a great reading experience into an even greater
learning opportunity with a Unit Study Curriculum Guide.
Available for select biographies.

Available from YWAM Publishing
1-800-922-2143 / www.ywampublishing.com